KU-507-572

Love for Love

an anthology of Love Poems

Love for Love

Edited by
John Burnside and Alec Finlay

pocketbooks
Morning Star Publications
Polygon

2000

Editorial concept © John Burnside, 2000.
Introduction © John Burnside, 2000.
Unless otherwise stated copyright remains with authors and artists, © 2000.
The acknowledgements on pages 196-197 constitutes an extension of this
copyright note.

Published by:
pocketbooks
Canongate Venture (5), New Street, Edinburgh EH8 8BH.

Morning Star Publications
Canongate Venture (5), New Street, Edinburgh EH8 8BH.

Polygon
22 George Square, Edinburgh EH8 9LF.

Typeset in Minion and Univers.
Designed by Lucy Richards and Matthew Chapman, with Alec Finlay.
Printed and bound by Redwood Books Limited, Trowbridge.

Printed on Munken Elk 90gsm available from Trebruk UK Limited.

Published with the assistance of a grant from the Scottish Arts Council National
Lottery Fund and a grant from Highlands & Islands Enterprise (HI Arts).

A CIP record is available from the British Library .

ISBN 0 7486 6276 6

pocketbooks 03

THE TRYST

O luely, luely cam she in
And luely she lay doun:
I kent her be her caller lips
And her breists sae sma' and roun'.

A' thru the nicht we spak nae word
Nor sinder'd bane frae bane:
A' thru the nicht I heard her hert
Gang soundin' wi' my ain.

It was about the waukrife hour
Whan cocks begin to craw
That she smool'd saftly thru the mirk
Afore the day wud daw.

Sae luely, luely, cam she in
Sae luely was she gaen
And wi' her a ' my simmer days
Like they had never been.

45

Typescript of William Soutar's *The Tryst*.
Reproduced by kind permission of the Trustees of the National Library of Scotland.

List of Contents

Love for love is the bargain with me
Robert Burns

Editors' Acknowledgements

The editors would like to thank the following people for their support in realising this project. Our thanks, firstly, to all of the contributors, who had to contend with the limited time available; and also to Cluny Sheeler, Thomas Evans and Andrew Phillip, who prepared the typescript and dealt with the permissions; Ken Cockburn and Alison Humphry of pocketbooks; Alison Bowden, Ian Davidson and Jeanie Scott at Polygon, and Andrew MacDougall at Scottish Book Source; Jess, for permission to use a detail from one of his collages on the front cover, and the Museum of Contemporary Art, Chicago, for kind permission to reproduce this; Norma Cole, for her help with this; the Trustees of the National Library of Scotland for permission to reproduce the typescript of William Soutar's 'The Tryst' as a frontispiece. We would also like to express our thanks to The Scottish Poetry Library which has been an invaluable resource in identifying poems, poets and publishers.

Introduction

For the opening of the fourth poem of his *Mythistorema* sequence, a poem about the Argonauts, that legendary group of friends and equals who joined Jason in his search for the elusive Golden Fleece, George Seferis evokes an image from the *Alcibiades*, one of Plato's minor dialogues:

And if the soul
is to know itself
it must look
into a soul:

In an extraordinarily economical way, these line express an essential truth about our condition. It is not merely the case that our lives are enriched by the exchanges and dialogues through which we engage with others, it is that we finally come into being when we address, and are addressed by, the other. Of course, these exchanges need not take the usual, that is, the obviously social, form; as readers – and writers – we can participate in continuing dialogues outside the limits of geographical and political space: we can speak to the dead, and we can hear their voices; we can share in lost days, and lost worlds; we can escape the limits of a given culture and ethics, and dwell for a time in the elsewhere. It is our good fortune that, through the written word, and especially through the lyric poem, we can engage in the most intimate dialogues – dialogues which transcend the social and the contingent – with distant strangers.

When we began work on this anthology, we decided that it was the spirit of these exchanges – these special forms of address – that we wanted the book to capture. Though it raised a number of interesting issues – chief of which, I suppose, was the question: what constitutes a love poem? – our approach was relatively simple. We invited a number of Scottish writers to choose a love poem, from any time and place, which had inspired, excited or influenced them in some way, whether directly or otherwise (the definition of 'love poem' was left entirely to the poets themselves). Alongside this poem, we asked each writer to place one of his or her own, preferably a new piece, though this was not essential. The new piece itself could, but need not necessarily, be a love poem. Again, the definition of this term was left to the poets – we did not expect, and certainly did not wish for, a whole anthology of the more conventional love poetry, and we were prepared for each writer's definition of that term to be a liberal one, from the kind of writing about romantic (and sometimes unrequited) love that might immediately spring to mind, to poems for children, or friends, or even beloved places, ideas, pursuits, or things.

As editors, we were most interested in what might arise from the correspondence element of the book. We wanted to encourage the invited writers to engage in – or rather, continue – a dialogue with those poets they admired, whether they were ancestors, or contemporaries, in new and interesting ways. A fine example of this type of correspondence came to mind in William Carlos Williams' poem, 'Address':

> To a look in my son's eyes –
> > I hope he did not see
> > > that I was looking –
> that I have seen
> > often enough
> > > in the mirror,
> a male look
> > approaching despair –
> > > there is a female look
> to match it
> > no need to speak of that:
> > > Perhaps

it was only a dreamy look
　　　　　not an unhappy one
　　　　　　　　　but absent
from the world –
　　　　　such as plagued the eyes
　　　　　　　　　of Bobby Burns
in his youth and threw him
　　　　　into the arms
　　　　　　　　　of women –
in which he could
　　　　　forget himself,
　　　　　　　　　not defiantly,
but with full acceptance
　　　　　of his lot
　　　　　　　　　as a man.
His Jean forgave him
　　　　　and took him to her heart
　　　　　　　　　time after time
when he would be
　　　　　too drunk
　　　　　　　　　with Scotch
or the love of other women
　　　　　to notice
　　　　　　　　　what he was doing.
What was he intent upon
　　　　　but to drown out
　　　　　　　　　that look? What
does it portend?
　　　　　A war
　　　　　　　　　will not erase it

nor a bank account,
        estlin,
                amounting to 9 figures.
Flow gently sweet Afton
        among thy green braes –
                no matter
that he wrote the song
        to another woman
                it was never for sale.

Here Williams, by way of a poem which overtly addresses both his son and the poet Robert Burns, recognises in his own heart a wildness, a force, a troublesome quality that might exist in the heart of any man. It is a poem that reminds us of a number of things: that the lyric has no business being politically, socially, or otherwise correct; that every poet works within a tradition which, when traced back, can be surprising in its origins; that the solitary act of walking a road, or sitting at a desk, composing a piece of poetry is always a part of a continuing dialogue, across time and space, with other writers, other readers.

Since I am speaking of origins, a few words of explanantion as to the origins of this present volume might be in order. The initial idea arose during a casual conversation I had with Alec Finlay over lunch one rainy afternoon in Edinburgh. To begin with, I saw it as an international project, or at least a project that would embrace the English-speaking world (on a personal level, I was particularly interested in dialogue between the 'old' world and the 'new'); for various reasons, however, we came to think of it – for the moment at least – as a Scottish anthology. While some of those reasons were practical and logistical (of the most obvious nature), there were other, more positive factors that contributed to the decision. One was that, at this point in our history, it struck us as worthwhile to consider the kinships and correspondences that exist between contemporary Scottish poets and their various influences. It felt interesting to work on a project which depended upon that essentially Scottish virtue of openness, of looking out to other cultures and traditions. The decision to concentrate on love poems originated, for me at least, in a weariness with the usual stereotypes of the Scots national character, especially that of the Scottish male, whether it was described as dour, narrow-minded and puritanical, or brutish, violent and insensitive. Of course, all stereotypes – especially those of 'national character' – should be treated with mistrust, if not open disdain; however, given the fact that such discussions were destined to continue, as this emerging nation strove to define itself, we wanted to suggest another, quite different image from the usual, tired, gritty-ugly or puritan-philistine one – an image which reveals the more tender, sensual and appreciative side of our character. It also seemed worthwhile, in contrast to our justly famous flyting tradition, to examine that other form of address for which Scots are known everywhere: given the standard preconceptions about the Scots 'national character', it may seem ironic perhaps, that some of the best-known love poems world-wide were composed by a Scot, but there is no need for anyone to stop at Burns in considering our gifts for the erotic, the justly-sentimental and the romantic.

Most important of all, however – beyond all political and national considerations – what interested me was to consider the nature of love, and of the love poem. In an age dominated by facts – and by the unreliability of the factual – what makes the love poem essential – what raises it to an almost magical valency – is the mystery at its centre. For in spite of the seeming dominance of the 'facts', love, whatever form it takes, is a mystery, and at least one of the reasons why we enter into love is that it creates a zone of mystery in our own lives. In this sense, the love poem is, by its very nature, a philosophical investigation, inextricably linked to the central epistemological question, the question of Being. Just as, for no obvious reason, the universe exists, so, for no obvious reason, we celebrate the ritual, the common miracle, of love. Love, like Being, does not belong to the world of ordinary discourse – that is, of rational or logical disquisition – for, like Being, it can only be spoken of obliquely, by way of metaphor or image. Love is the most obvious manifestation of the interconnectedness of everything: as Plato – and Seferis – tell us, we do not come fully into being other than in our (loving) relations with the other.

For this reason, the love poem, whatever form it takes, performs a valuable spiritual function, by continually reminding us that there is a huge chasm between the ways in which we are identified in our everyday transactions and the ways in which love describes us. At the most fundamental level, love calls us back from the realm of the merely factual to the mystery of the real. This is the true function of the love poem: to remind us of who we are, and who we are capable of being; while our everyday social roles define us as persons, love reminds us that we are also souls. It is for this reason, more than any other, that we present this tangle of love poems, by writers both living and dead, speaking across cultures and traditions, across time and space, in a constant and necessary renewal of the world we inhabit, and the language we use to describe it.

John Burnside

The Love Poems

Edwin Morgan

Wild Nights

Wild Nights – Wild Nights!
Were I with thee
Wild Nights should be
Our luxury!

Futile – the Winds –
To a Heart in port –
Done with the Compass –
Done with the Chart!

Rowing in Eden –
Ah, the Sea!
Might I but moor – Tonight –
In Thee!

Emily Dickinson

The Persistence of Love

What is this picture but a fragment?
Is it linen – papyrus – who can say?
All those stains and fents and stretched bits, but
she was a character, even a beauty, you can see that
from the set of her head and the rakish snood
her tight black curls are fighting to escape from.
She is wearing a very very pale violet tunic
which is partly transparent, partly translucent,
partly not there. It has slipped off one shoulder
but the shoulder has gone. The other arm has faded
to a scarcely perceptible gesture. One sandal
gleams. All the rest is conjecture.
Her name is a letter or two: Sa, Saf –
O she is all fragments. There she is though!

Edwin Morgan

Robin Robertson

She Moved Through the Fair

My young love said to me, "My brothers won't mind,
And my parents won't slight you for your lack of kind."
Then she stepped away from me, and this she did say,
"It will not be long, love, till our wedding day."

She stepped away from me and she moved through the fair,
And fondly I watched her go here and go there,
Then she went her way homeward with one star awake,
As the swan in the evening moves over the lake.

The people were saying no two were e'er wed
But one had a sorrow that never was said,
And I smiled as she passed with her goods and her gear,
And that was the last that I saw of my dear.

I dreamt it last night that my young love came in,
So softly she entered, her feet made no din;
She came close beside me, and this she did say,
"It will not be long love, till our wedding day."

Padraic Colum

Head over Heels

Holding hands on the big wheel
fifty feet above the Tuileries'
evening jasmine, I loved
your play at fear,
my brave stab at insouciance,
the way the bright circuitry of Paris
lay beneath us like the night sky,
like the plan of our lives.

Robin Robertson

Robert Crawford

Marion Angus
    The Faithful Heart

Robert Crawford
    The Click

The Faithful Heart

There cam' a man from Brig o' Feugh,
Whaur I was wild and young;
I kent him by his heather step
And the turn upon his tongue.

He spak' o' crofters on the hill,
The shepherd from the fauld,
Simmers wi' the flourish sweet,
Winters dour and cauld;

O' this guid man and that guid wife,
Aince lads and lassies brave,
Hoo ane still whustles at the ploo'
And ane is in his grave;

O' them that's ower the faemy seas,
And them that bides at hame,
But I socht nae news o' my auld love
Nor named her bonnie name.

Marion Angus

The Click

for Alice

Walking with you in the Elysian Fields of Paris.
You sat by the pool. The fountain. The metal chair.

I used my camera as a prayer, its answer
Light from water, from the silvery chairlegs, the sky

Silkening around you, where you sat smiling,
Wearing that city like a second wedding-dress. Click.

Robert Crawford

Christopher Whyte

Jaime Gil de Biedma
  Vals del Aniversario
  translated by Christopher Whyte

Christopher Whyte
  An Aiteigin, An Oisean Dhe Mo Bhith
  translated by Gavin Bowd

Vals del Aniversario

Nada hay tan dulce como una habitación
para dos, cuando ya no nos queremos demasiado,
fuera de la ciudad, en un hotel tranquilo,
y parejas dudosas y algún niño con ganglios,

si no es esta ligera sensación
de irrealidad. Algo como el verano
en casa de mis padres, hace tiempo,
como viajes en tren por la noche. Te llamo

para decir que no te digo nada
que tú ya no conozcas, o si acaso
para besarte vagamente
los mismos labios.

Has dejado el balcón.
Ha oscurecido el cuarto
mientras que no miramos tiernamente, incómodos
de no sentir el peso de tres años.

Todo es igual, parece
que no fue ayer. Y este sabor nostálgico,
que los silencios ponen en la boca,
posiblemente induce a equivocarnos

en nuestros sentimientos. Pero no
sin alguna riserva, porque por debajo
algo tira más fuerte y es (para decirlo
quizá de un modo menos inexacto)

dificil recordar que nos queremos,
si no es con cierta imprecisión, y el sábado,
que es hoy, queda tan cerca
de ayer a última hora y de pasado

mañana
por la mañana . . .

Jaime Gil de Biedma

Anniversary Waltz

Nothing can be as sweet as a room
for two, now that our love is no longer excessive,
outside the city, in a quiet hotel,
with suspicious-looking couples and gangling children,

except this faint sense of
irreality. Rather like summer
in my parents' house, long ago,
or travelling by train at night. I call you

to tell you that I have nothing to tell you
you do not know already, or perhaps
absent-mindedly to kiss
those same lips of yours.

You have come in from the balcony.
The room has grown dark
as we look at one another tenderly, embarrassed
not to feel the weight of three years.

Nothing has changed, it could
have been yesterday. And this nostalgic tang
silence places in the mouth
might just be causing us to mistake

the nature of our feelings. But not
without reservations, because down below
something pulls more strongly and (perhaps
this is a less vague way of putting it)

it is hard to remember that we love each other
without a degree of impreciisiony, and Saturday,
which is today, is no less near
than last thing last night, or the day

after tomorrow tomorrow
morning . . .

translated by Christopher Whyte

An Àiteigin, An Oisean Dhe Mo Bhith

An àiteigin, an oisean dhe mo bhith,
tha i fhathast maireann, an aisling sin

gun coinnich sinn le chèile anns a' bhaile
ghrianach, rèidh, an ceann bliadhna no dhà,

is leus an là ann mar gum biodh a' phlanaid
ga glacadh ann an truinnsear de dh'airgead

chun a lainnir is a neart gu lèir
a chruinneachadh, gun anbharr no gairge,

oir cha bhi boinne fliche anns an adhar,
is giùlainidh na daoin' an teas gun strì.

Rachainn a chadal leis na h-uinneagan
làn-fhosgailte, is nochdadh tu san leabaidh

gun eòlas dhomh, oir b' annsa leat bhith anmoch,
is nuair a thòisicheadh an là a' bristeadh

dh'èiricheadh tu, mar dhuine bhios a' triall
gun dùsgadh, gus na còmhlaichean a dhùnadh,

's tiughad a thoirt air ais don dorchadas,
air neo bhitheadh a' chamhanach gad bhuaireadh.

Dh'fhanainn car sealain is mo shùilean fosgailt',
's mo chuimhn' a' dol air grad-theàrnadh na h-oidhche

sa cheàrnaig mhòir, is mi 'nam shuidh' a' coimhead
air siubhal deireannach nan corra-bàn.

Christopher Whyte

Somewhere In A Corner Of My Being

Somewhere in a corner of my being
there still exists the dream

we'll meet again a year from now
in the sunny and flat city

where daylight is as if the planet
had been caught in a silver plate

to gather all its strength and brilliance
without any excess or harshness

for there the air is never humid
and people live happy in the heat.

At night the windows would be wide open
and you would appear in the bed

imperceptibly, always late,
and when the day began to break,

you would rise, like someone walking
in their sleep, to close the shutters,

and restore density to the darkness,
knowing that twilight disturbs you.

I'd stay for a while with my eyes open,
remembering the sudden falling of night

in the great square, where I sat and watched
the last flight of the storks.

Christopher Whyte

translated by Gavin Bowd

Ian Hamilton Finlay

The Immoral Proposition

If you never do anything for anyone else
you are spared the tragedy of human relation-

ships. If quietly and like another time
there is the passage of an unexpected thing:

to look at it is more
than it was. God knows

nothing is competent nothing is
all there is. The unsure

egoist is not
good for himself.

Robert Creeley

For Pia

Your needle-and-thread
in the sail of my Zulu.

Ian Hamilton Finlay
Zulu, a type of fishing vessel – in this case a model.

John Glenday

The Tryst

O luely, luely, cam she in
And luely she lay doun:
I kent her be her caller lips
And her breists sae sma' and roun'.

A' thru the nicht we spak nae word
Nor sinder'd bane frae bane:
A' thru the nicht I heard her hert
Gang soundin' wi' my ain.

It was about the waukrife hour
Whan cocks begin to craw
That she smool'd saftly thru the mirk
Afore the day wud daw.

Sae luely, luely, cam she in
Sae luely was she gaen;
And wi' her a' my simmer days
Like they had never been.

William Soutar

Landscape With Flying Man

I read about him that was given wings.
His father fixed those wings to carry him away.

They carried him half way home, and then he fell.
And he fell not because he flew,

but because he loved it so. You see,
it's neither pride, nor gravity but love

that in the end will pull us back down to the world.
Love furnishes the wings, and that same love

will watch over us as we drown.
The soul makes a thousand crossings; the heart, just one.

John Glenday

Tom Leonard

William Cowper
  To Mary Unwin

Tom Leonard
  touching your face

To Mary Unwin

The twentieth year is wellnigh past
Since first our sky was overcast;
Ah would that this might be the last!
    My Mary!

Thy spirits have a fainter flow,
I see thee daily weaker grow –
'Twas my distress that brought thee low,
    My Mary!

Thy needles, once a shining store,
For my sake restless heretofore,
Now rust disused, and shine no more;
    My Mary!

For though thou gladly wouldst fulfil
The same kind office for me still,
Thy sight now seconds not thy will,
    My Mary!

But well thou play'dst the housewife's part,
And all thy threads with magic art
Have wound themselves about this heart,
    My Mary!

Thy indistinct expressions seem
Like language utter'd in a dream;
Yet me they charm, whate'er the theme,
    My Mary!

Thy silver locks, once auburn bright,
Are still more lovely in my sight
Than golden beams of orient light,
    My Mary!

For could I view nor them nor thee,
What sight worth seeing could I see?
The sun would rise in vain for me,
    My Mary!

Partakers of thy sad decline
Thy hands their little force resign;
Yet gently press'd, press gently mine,
    My Mary!

Such feebleness of limbs thou prov'st
That now at every step thou mov'st
Upheld by two; yet still thou lov'st,
    My Mary!

And still to love, though press'd with ill,
In wintry age to feel no chill,
With me is to be lovely still,
    My Mary!

But ah! by constant heed I know
How oft the sadness that I show
Transforms thy smiles to looks of woe,
    My Mary!

And should my future lot be cast
With much resemblance of the past,
Thy worn-out heart will break at last –
    My Mary!

William Cowper

touching your face

with that
silence

it creates
allowing

and
trusting

the allowed;
all that's

been said
and is saying

this time
breath

held
between us

each time
familiar

each time
new

Tom Leonard

Andrew Greig

The Leaving

I light a candle
for your coming back,

brilliant and frail
in a darkening room.

Beautiful it is, and damned
not to last, only endure.

Almost as fragile
as darkness itself.

John Glenday

A Shuttered Lantern

And when she goes she takes with her
a shuttered lantern.

Wherever you think of her inhabiting –
work, her children, bars
and friends – stays dark.
The light falls only on her face
as you last saw it.

And when she writes she must learn
to make love to him with more attention,
do more than follow the motion of his kiss,
you blink at the first glimpse
of a light that will blind you
when she raises the lamp's side
and vanishes.

Andrew Greig

Frank Kuppner

Sorley Maclean
   from Poems to Eimhir
   translated by Iain Crichton Smith

Frank Kuppner
   Halves

Girl of the yellow, heavy-yellow, gold-yellow hair,
the tune of your lips and Europe's pain together.
Lustrous, ringletted, joyful, beautiful lass,
our time's shame would not infect your kiss.

Can the music of your beauty hide from me
the ominous discord in this harmony?
The rampant thief and brute at Europe's head,
the ancient songs, your lips so proud and red.

Can a body's whiteness and a forehead's sun
conceal that impudent treachery from my brain –
spite of the bourgeoisie, poison of its creed,
a dismal Scotland, feeble and weak-kneed?

Can beauty and the mendacity of verse
deceive the patient with its transient cures
or hide the Spanish miner from his doom,
his soul going down without delerium?

What is your kiss, electrical and proud,
when valued by each drop of precious blood
that fell on the frozen mountain-sides of Spain
when men were dying in their bitter pain?

What is each ringlet of your golden hair
when weighed against that poverty and fear
which Europe's people bear and still must bear
from the first slave-ship to slavery entire?

Sorley Maclean   translated by Iain Crichton Smith

Halves

(A sonnet mistranslated from the author's own Albanian)

Girl of the green-gold, red-gold, pink-gold nexnox,
how much more proud is the gold that lies in your nixnux,
than the gold in the sky of morning over, for instance, Balshagray Avenue
which the cars thunder down to the tunnel under the Clyde.

What do I care that in more prestigious cities
finer avenues are full of finer vehicles – if they are;
it matters less than the coffee you offered me this morning,
but, alas, completely forgot to pour out before you left once more.

It reminded me of how once, much too early, I arrived
in the waiting area of the local airport, and, sitting down there,
noticed a half-empty plastic coffee container under the seat next to mine.

Perhaps, I thought, the other half of that congealed beverage
is moulding itself to part of a body travelling through the skies,
or is in another continent already, unseen and silently altering.

Frank Kuppner

Tracey Herd

John Berryman
  from The Dream Songs (147)

Tracey Herd
  He'll Have To Go

Dream Song (147)

Henry's mind grew blacker the more he thought.
He looked onto the world like the act of an aged whore.
Delmore, Delmore.
He flung to pieces and they hit the floor.
Nothing was true but what Marcus Aurelius taught,
'All that is foul smell and blood in a bag.'

He lookt on the world like the leavings of a hag.
Almost his love died from him, any more.
His mother & William
were vivid in the same mail Delmore died.
The world is lunatic. This is the last ride.
Delmore, Delmore.

High in the summer branches the poet sang.
His throat ached, and he could sing no more.
All ears closed
across the heights where Delmore and Gertrude sprang
so long ago, in the goodness of which it was composed.
Delmore, Delmore!

John Berryman

He'll Have To Go

I'm sitting in an empty restaurant,
Dressed up to the nines, but I might
As well be invisible, or wearing
Another's face. It feels later

Than it really is, and darker. A cold
Dark place, where you are always absent
Without apology. That night, I bought myself
An hour's grace and I've been paying

For it ever since. The plates are cracked,
The tables bare. Somewhere, a record
I didn't ask for begins to play. You are
At home, still sitting in that chair, lost

In your music while I search everywhere.
Four Walls, He'll Have to Go.
Father, I've sent all the boys away
And still you won't come back to me.

Tracey Herd

Matthew Hollis

No Choice

I think about you
in as many ways as rain comes.

(I am growing, as I get older,
to hate metaphors – their exactness
and their inadequacy.)

Sometimes these thoughts are
a moistness, hardly falling, than which
nothing is more gentle:
sometimes, a rattling shower, a
bustling Spring-cleaning of the mind:
sometimes, a drowning downpour.

I am growing, as I get older,
to hate metaphor,
to love gentleness,
to fear downpours.

Norman MacCaig

In You More Than You

the lines of a lifetime gather like water.
In places these streams are a torrent,
a raging flood, a sweeping away;
in places a careful shallow, a rockpool
still as a mirror. What I see in you is me:
an image of myself complete, as one,
more real than I could ever be.
What I see in you I cannot live to,
too much the perfect picture of myself.
So I will part, and leave to you
the fragments of the me I seem,
this hem of guesses and glue. I'm not
the me I thought I was, and tell you so.
Pass round the pieces and let them go.

Matthew Hollis

Anne Macleod

Nina Cassian
    Temptation
    translated by Brenda Walker and Andrea Delatant

Anne Macleod
    Nights Like These

Temptation

Call yourself alive? Look, I promise you
that for the first time you'll feel your pores opening
like fish mouths, and you'll actually be able to hear
your blood surging through all those lanes,
and you'll feel light gliding across the cornea
like the train of a dress. For the first time
you'll be aware of gravity
like a thorn in your heel,
and your shoulder blades will ache for want of wings.
Call yourself alive? I promise you
you'll be deafened by dust falling on the furniture,
you'll feel your eyebrows turning to two gashes,
and every memory you have – will begin
at Genesis.

Nina Cassian   translated by Brenda Walker and Andrea Delatant

Nights Like These

nights like these, I wonder
why we ever did it – talked –
fucked – kissed – I wonder if
we ever did it
or if
it were all imagined lyric
– scoured mythology

is that not history, is that not song?

nights like these, flesh wisening

Anne Macleod

Stewart Conn

.

Ettrick

When we first rade down Ettrick,
Our bridles were ringing, our hearts were dancing,
The waters were singing, the sun was glancing,
An' blithely our voices rang out thegither,
As we brushed the dew frae the blooming heather,
   When we first rade down Ettrick.

When we next rade down Ettrick,
The day was dying, the wild birds calling,
The wind was sighing, the leaves were falling,
An' silent an' weary, but close thegither,
We urged our steeds through the faded heather,
   When we next rade down Ettrick.

When I last rade down Ettrick,
The winds were shifting, the storm was waking,
The snow was drifting, the heart was breaking,
For we never again were to ride thegither,
In sun or storm on the mountain heather,
   When I last rade down Ettrick.

Lady John Scott

In the Museum of Scotland

I come across a white horse in a glass case,
decked with period artifacts each in its place:
saddle studs and plates, silvered harness junctions,
slivers of body armour, and from muzzle to ear
ornate fragments of chamfron – not as a work of art
but displaying each item's ancient function.
Going to bed that night, I cannot but wonder
what of your 'you-ness' might be deduced
from the strewn scarves, the array of bracelets
on the dressing table, the jet and greenstone beads;
and what of custom and appearance, in those items
spilling from your wardrobe, could be implanted
in the mind of someone who did not know you.
My good fortune lies in having no need
of such accoutrements to conjure up
the warmth and gracefulness they enhance,
the living likeness of their milk-white steed.

Stewart Conn

Robert Creeley
    Love Comes Quietly

Thomas A. Clark
    when I look at you

Love Comes Quietly

Love comes quietly,
finally, drops
about me, on me,
in the old ways.

What did I know
thinking myself
able to go
alone all the way.

Robert Creeley

when I look at you
you look away
I look away
when you look at me

here we are together
the blackthorn is in bloom
it is as it has always been
nothing is the same

if the glances are entangled
bindweed, rose briar, vetch
the first days, first inscriptions
are restored at a touch

Thomas A. Clark

Janet Paisley

Ted Hughes
   Bridestones, West Yorkshire

Janet Paisley
   Lost Heroes

Bridestones, West Yorkshire

Holy of holies – a hill-top chapel.
Actually a crown of outcrop rock –
Earth's heart-stuff laid bare.

Crowding congregation of skies.
Tense congregation of hills.
You do nothing casual here.

The wedding stones
Are electrified with whispers.

And marriage is nailed down
By this slender-necked, heavy-handed
Black exclamation mark
Of rock.

And you go
With the wreath of the weather
The wreath of the hills
The wreath of stars
Upon your shoulders.

And from now on,
The sun
Touches you
With the shadow of this finger.

From now on
The moon stares into your skull
From this perch.

Ted Hughes

Lost Heroes

Maybe we were right to cherish you,
the axeman rushing in, fearing no wolf.

In those giant days, you were the forearm
solid as a tree-limb hoisting us up.
The great boom of your voice cleared
our path, made landfall safe. Your great fist
a champion we'd field to any threat,
heartbeat the hammock of our rest.
Sheltered by your shadow, we'd cry
a storm knowing you'd settle it. Had you
wept the world would have fragmented.

Rising on the wings you lent us
we did not look back, see your feet
shackled to solid earth, deep rooted
in circumstance. If we dance now
it's on your many deaths: sickness first
to find you out, famine to leave you unfed.
War always took you. And when at last
the lifeboats came, above pity the sound,
your voice saying Go. Go on, go ahead.

Janet Paisley

Anonymous (Medieval Irish)
Líadan and Cuithir
translated by James Carney

Rody Gorman
Beinn MoGhaoil
version by Iain S. Mac a' Phearsain

Líadan and Cuirithir

No pleasure
that deed I did, tormenting him,
tormenting what I treasure.

Joyfully
but that God had come between us then
had I granted what I begged of me.

Not unwise
is the way that he is taking now,
enduring pain and gaining Paradise.

Great folly
where once I showed such gentleness
to set Cuirithir against me!

Líadan I;
they say that I loved Cuirithir,
nor would I, if I could, deny.

The while I bless
that I was in his company
and was treating him with tenderness.

A woodland breeze
was my melody with Cuirithir
sounding harmony of reddening seas.

It seemed thus:
the last thing I would ever do
was a deed to come between us.

Cry clearly:
if any lovers this heart cherishes,
he its darling, loved most dearly

A cry of pain
and the heart within was rent in two,
without him never beats again.

Anonymous (Medieval Irish)   translated by James Carney

Seadh, a Bheinn MoGhaoil ud,
San robh mi eòlach uair
'S tu air tòiseachadh air leaghadh
As dèidh nam mìltean air mhìltean
De bhliadhnaichean de reothadh,

Saoil gu dè na marbhain
A thig ris fod uachdar
A rèir is mar a thèid
An leaghadh air adhart 's an t-aiteamh,
A rinn sreap ri do dhealbh
Is ri do chruth, na gaisgich,
'S nach d' ràinig am binnean a riamh,
Nan laighe beul fodha shìos mun a' bhall
Far an do thuit iad, air an call?

Rody Gorman

Beinn MoGhaoil

Yes, Beinn MoGhaoil
I once knew
having begun to melt
after millenia and millenia
of glacial years

I wonder what corpses will appear
under your surface
as receding thaw progresses,
those who climbed your face,
your form,
the darling ones
that never reached the summit
lying face down at your base
where they fell bewildered?

Rody Gorman   version by Iain S. Mac a' Phearsain

Ian Stephen

Norman Malcolm MacDonald
    Mor

Ian Stephen
    How Many Kinds of Love

Mor

I eat

salt herring

with my fingers

read a story of

Hebrides Fisheries

my love

has salted

my potatoes

she puts peas

on my white plate

Norman Malcolm MacDonald

How Many Kinds of Love

How many kinds of love come from the pans?
Liver and bacon swam deep in tomatoes,
baking, waiting, if or when I'd come.
She'd hope for conversation when I sat.

But it won't be turkey like your mother's.
The melting lamb cut deep
with sticks of rosemary
rampant as bracken on
the height that faces Sunart.
Or the thyme Denise plucked from the Ross
to leaven a perched beanstew
by a Sound that thought it was Moroccan
as we burned like David Balfour on the rock.

Between one person's cardiac, one's cancer,
the carnal shapes of rocks at Rackwick Bay
till you bit at me for fingering
the smokey from the bone then
casting that and skin to skuas.
It's how we eat fish here.
And I went sullen as your
salts were drying on my skin.

Now you, my love, boil the bootlace conger,
tight ling, skinned monks
till the broth is separate from the debris
and it's all red as the bleed of
a fresh burn to a Greek Atlantic sea.

Ian Stephen

Alexander Montgomerie
  from The Secreit Prais of Love

Colin Donati
  Love as the Ens Realissimum

from The Secreit Prais of Love

Suppose the hevins be huge for to behold,
      Contening all within thair compas wyde,
The starris in time, thoght tedious, may be told;
      Becaus within a certan bounds they byde:
      The carde the earth from waters may devyde:
But who is he can limit love, I wene,
Quhom nather carde nor compas can contene?

Quhat force is this, subdueing all and sum?
      Quhat force is this that maks the tygris tame?
Quhat force is this that na man can ouircum?
      Quhat force is this that richtlie nane can name?
      Quhat force is this that careis sic a fame? –
A vehemency that words can not reveill
Quhilk I conclude to suffer and conceill.

Alexander Montgomerie

Love as the Ens Realissimum

(aftir the manner of Montgomerie)

Suppose all stars in every airt we see
      Thru all the heavins, owir large to comprehend,
And all the earths in which things born mon die,
      All prinklin signals worlds receive and send,
      All gravity that gars the space to bend,
And every galaxy baith far and near
Suld rise up at a snap and disappear,

Love waldna be destroyed in this event,
      Love wald bide on, the ens that stairts again,
Love wald bide on to mak new argument,
      Love wald bide on, naething could it distrain,
      Love wald bide on that nou is seen by nane,
A secret seid concealed in ben the hairt,
Whilk Christ sayd is aye hail in every pairt.

Colin Donati

Christine De Luca

True Ways of Knowing

Not an ounce excessive, not an inch too little,
Our easy reciprocations. You let me know
The way a boat would feel, if it could feel,
The intimate support of water.

The news you bring me has been news forever,
So that I understand what a stone would say
If only a stone could speak. Is it sad a grassblade
Can't know how it is lovely?

Is it sad that you can't know, except by hearsay
(My gossiping failing words) that you are the way
A water is that can clench its palm and crumple
A boat's confiding timbers?

But that's excessive, and too little. Knowing
The way a circle would describe its roundness,
We touch two selves and feel, complete and gentle,
The intimate support of being.

The way that flight would feel a bird flying
(If it could feel) is the way a space that's in
A stone that's in a water would know itself
If it had our way of knowing.

Norman MacCaig

Into your knowingness

These images are as elegant as maths proofs,
as elemental: water, stone, the circle of infinite
self-knowledge. They encompass touch, that
shared coordinate; and in true ways of knowing
reproach reciprocation that's sparing, tentative.
I reach into the spaces of our squandered silence,
into our grassblade moments, and wonder
at your knowingness that predates the naming
of all actions, all intentions; into a time when,
in primal innocence, you stalked and killed,
bore home the gifts with crushing diligence.
But that's excessive and too little. I will
draw lines around your purest meanings
and step into that gentle circle still.

Christine De Luca

Johann Wolfgang Goethe
from Venetian Epigrams
translated by Ken Cockburn

Ken Cockburn
Elm Row

36.

Müde war ich geworden, nur immer Gemälde zu sehen,
    Herrliche Schätze der Kunst, wie sie Venedig bewahrt.
Denn auch dieser Genuß verlangt Erholung und Muße;
    Nach lebendigem Reiz suchte mein schmachtender Blick.
Gauklerin! da ersah ich in dir zu den Bübchen das Urbild,
    Wie sie Johannes Bellin reizend mit Flügeln gemalt,
Wie sie Paul Veronese mit Bechern dem Bräutigam sendet,
    Dessen Gäste, getäuscht, Wasser genießen für Wein.

139.

Zürnet nicht, ihr Frauen, daß wir das Mädchen bewundern:
    Ihr genießet des Nachts, was sie am Abend erregt.

158.

Ach! sie neiget das Haupt, die holde Knospe, wer gießet
    Eilig erquickendes Naß neben die Wurzel ihr hin?
Daß sie froh sich entfalte, die schönen Stunden der Blüte
    Nicht zu frühe vergehn, endlich auch reife die Frucht.
Aber auch mir – mir sinket das Haupt von Sorgen und Mühe.
    Liebes Mädchen! Ein Glas schäumenden Weines herbei.

Johann Wolfgang Goethe (1790)

36.
Tired, I was, of seeing painting after painting,
masterpieces, and Venice isn't short of these.
This type of pleasure too requires a break, a breather;
wearied, my gaze went seeking livelier delights.
Acrobat! I saw it was you behind those figures
which Bellini depicts so charmingly with wings,
which Veronese sends with goblets to the bridegroom;
fooled, his wedding-guests drink water as if it were wine.

139.
Don't be angry, ladies, if the girl attracts us;
you enjoy at night what, earlier, she has aroused.

158.
See how her head is drooping, wilting, the sweet young thing,
    and who is there
able to pour, as of now, some goodness over her roots?
If she can open with joy, and the beauties of her blossom
aren't forced on, hothoused, the fruit will surely grow ripe.
As for me – my head is weary with cares of its own.
Sweetheart, here! Bring me a glass of sparkling wine.

translated by Ken Cockburn

Elm Row

The waitress brings me *un americano*.
Bittersweet. Before me, its spine cracked,
the pages yellowing, your *Epigramme*,
read *in situ*, back in '86;

mercurially composed, creating a balance
in the rush of revolution and of love
as irresistable as the *acqua alta*
– the broken beds that were Christiane's gift –

the waitress moves her grace across the room,
could she turn water into wine? – remember
another, *there's a face you'd leave home for*, a friend

remarked, and remember Pound's grave, a chance find,
that day of the fireworks above Salute; later,
night filled with the benevolence of rain.

Ken Cockburn

Robert Alan Jamieson

Briodal Mathar

Mo luran thu
mo dhuinein thu,
èh, m' ultachan is m' eallach cléibh;
s tu luchd sàibhir
nan long Spainteach,
sìod an àird riu s lion fo ghreis.

M' Osgar mór thu
m' usgar oír thu,
mo mhogul chnó a chromas geug;
lìonadh cupain,
riarach' guidhe,
críoch mo shiubhail, freagairt m' fheum;

Leabaidh éirigh
do mo ghréin thu,
ìul mo cheum thu thar gach reul;
cuilean suairc thu
faillean uain thu
fearan cruaidh thig gu bhith treun.

Deòrsa mac Iain Deòrsa

Mother's Fondling Talk

My bonny thing art thou, my mannie art thou – eh, my arm load and breast burden; thou art the rich lading of the Spanish ships, silk aloft on them and linen embroidered.

My great Oscar art thou, my golden jewel, my cluster of nuts that curves the bough; my cup filling, my prayer-fulfilment, end of my journeying, answer to my need.

The bed from which my sun rises art thou, the guidance of my steps more than every star; a pleasant puppy art thou, a green shoot, a hardy wee man who will come to be strong.

George Campbell Hay

It took a lifetime to realise

Love is not blindly forgetting others
    and swopping better selves for worse.

Nor is it a sudden churning of the stomach
    or that lumping of the bone-dry throat.

Love is a constant singing in the heart
    and the feeling you may shortly fly.

It's that we're finally forgiving of the bad
    in our selves and our others too.

It's then we are ready to begin afresh
    driven by emotion as the green sea

rising, surely breaking on a ready shore
    from the deep of the ocean's well

You are that wave rising now
    breaking, breaking

        white on an ashen coast
           deafening then silent

Robert Alan Jamieson

aonghas macneacail

Dòmhnall Ruadh Choruna
   from An Eala Bhan / The Fair Swan
   translated by Fred Macaulay

aonghas macneacail
   gridlock agus gaol / gridlock and love

Gur duilich leam mar tha mi,
'S mo chridhe 'n sàs aig bròn
Bhon an uair a dh'fhàg mi
Beanntan àrd a' cheò,
Gleanntannan a' mhànrain,
Nan loch, nam bàgh's nan sròm,
'S an eala bhàn tha tàmh ann
Gach là air bheil mi 'n tòir.

Tha mise 'n seo 's mo shùil an iar
On chrom a' ghrian san t-sàl;
Mo dhùrachd leig mi às a dèidh
Ged fhios am faic mi màireach i
Nuair dhìreas i gu h-àrd,
Is iomairt lann gu bhith ri chèil'
Nuair 's lèir dhuinn beul an là.

Tha 'n talamh lèir mun cuairt dhiom
Na mheal lan suas 's na neòil
Aig na shells a' bualadh –
Cha lèir dhomh bhuam le ceò;
Gun chlaisneachd aig mo chluasan
Le fuaim a' ghunna mhòir;
Ach ged tha 'n uair seo cruaidh orm,
Tha mo smuaintean air NicLeòid.

Ach ma thig an t-àm
Is anns an Fhraing gu faigh mi bàs,
'S san uaigh gun tèid mo shìneadh
Far eil na mìltean chàch,
Mo bheannachd leis a' ghruagaich,
A' chaileag uasal bhàn –
Gach là a dh'fhalbh gun uallach dhi,
Gun nàire gruaidh na dhàil.

Oidhche mhath leat fhèin, a rùin,
Nad leabaidh chùbhraidh bhlàth;
Cadal sàmhach air a' chùl
'S do dhùsgadh sunndach slàn.
Tha mise 'n seo san truinnsidh fhuair
'S nam chluasan fuaim a' bhàis,
Gun dùil ri faighinn às le buaidh –
'S tha 'n cuan cho buan ri shnàmh.

Dòmhnall Ruadh Choruna

The Fair Swan

I feel desolate,
my heart seared by sorrow,
since I left
the high misty hills,
the beguiling glens
of loch, bay and strome,
and the fair swan who stays there
and I pursue unceasingly.

I am here gazing westwards
since the sun sank in the sea.
I took my sincere farewell of her,
feeling she left me too soon
and not knowing if I shall see her again tomorrow
as she rises skywards,
for battle will be joined
when we see the glimmer of day.

Around me massive quantities of earth
are being blown sky-high.
I cannot see far
for the smoke of bursting shells.
My ears are completely deafened
by the big guns,
but though the situation is intolerable,
my thoughts are of NicLeòid.

But should it happen
that I am killed in France
and laid in the grave
as thousands are already,
my blessings go with the maiden,
so fair and elegant.
May her every day be free of care
and her life a source of pride.

Goodnight, my love,
in your warm fragrant bed,
a quiet sleep to you
and a joyous wholesome awakening.
I am here in a cold trench,
the sounds of death constantly in my ears,
with little hope of emerging victorious,
and the sea is too wide to swim.

(verses 1, 3, 4, 12, 13) translated by Fred Macauley

air leathad na drochaid,
a suidhe na mo chàr, gun ghluasad,
ann an cuan de ghlainne 's stàilinn,
cinn feirge 's foighidinn
tromh na h-uinneagan, gun ghluasad,
ag èisdeachd ris an rèidio
naidheachdan an latha
's fòn astaigh, na guthan maotha
ùghdarrasach a cumail stiùir
air beachd is ceist, is
mise seo, nam chàr, gun ghluasad,
mar a tha gach ceann mun cuairt orm,
mar phrìosanaich nar ceallan dùrdail
ghlainne 's stàilinn, ag èisdeachd
ris an rèidio, na guthan maotha
cumail smachd air smuaint, ach
siud, mar chlaidheamh briathrach
mòr, a sgudadh chinn nam maoth,
the guth na feirge 'g èirigh a
fòn-siùbhlach glaist an cuan de
ghlainne 's stàilinn, fòs gun ghluasad,
ged a tha e gluasad mhonaidhean
de bhialachd is de bhriag, toirt
anail as na guthan maotha, gaoir
a chuthaich lasrach as an rèidio,

bu siud an eas de dhìtidhean,
ach thàinig e gu tàmh, is ann an
sgàil' an smuaint gun ghairm e
gaol da chèile, *prìosanach gu bheil mi*
anns an reothairt reòta seo, tha sinne
dlùth, is bì, is chunnaic mi, air gnùis
nam prìosanach, nan ceallan teann
de ghlainne 's stàillinn, fiamh a ghàire
is leig mi fhìn mo smuaint an àird,
mar cholman gaoil, gu ruig e thu
gu ruig e thu

aonghas macneacail

gridlock and love

on the brae of the bridge,
sitting in my car, not moving,
in a sea of glass and steel,
of furious and patient heads
through windows, not moving,
listening to the radio,
the daily news, a phone-in, bland
authoritative voices steer
each question and reply, and
i am here, in my car, not moving,
like every head around me,
all prisoners in purring cells
of glass and steel, listening
to the radio, bland voices
steering thought, but
then, a verbal claymore
slicing off bland heads,
the voice of fury rises from
a mobile phone imprisoned in
a sea of glass and steel, still
not moving, though that voice
shifts mountainsides of
lies and plausibilities and takes
the breath from those bland voices,
pain of fury flaming on the radio,
a wild cascade of condemnation,

then the anger ebbs, and in
the shade of thought, declares a
love for partner, *prisoner i may be*
in this frozen tide, but we stay
close, and now i see each other
prisoned face, in each closed cell
of glass and steel, break into smiles
and now i let my own thoughts rise
like doves, to fly toward you, love,
to fly toward you, love

aonghas macneacail

Gael Turnbull

Robert Garioch
   Ghaisties

Gael Turnbull
   Amorous Greetings

Ghaisties

Cauld are the ghaisties in yon kirkyaird,
    and cauld the airms
that they mell wi the mists of the timm breists of their loves;
at the heid of their bed cauld angels staund on guaird,
    and marble doves.
They ken-na the fear of Gode, as they sleep ayont sin,
    nor the terror of man,
and there's nane but the angels to glunch at their true loves' chairms,
yet they lang for the reek of the creeshie swat frae the skin
    and the grup of a haun.
But we in the warld are alowe
wi the glawmer of bluid-reid flame
that loups to the bluid in yer tongue's tip as it tingles on mine,
    and the howe
of the back we love wi our finger-nebbs, and the wame,
brent-white, wi a flush aneath like cramosie wine,
hou it curves to meet my ain!
    O, ma sonsie frow,
whit tho the flesh be bruckle, and fiends be slee,
the joys of the solid earth we'll pree or they dwine,
we'll lauch at daith, and man, and the fiend, aa three,
    afore we dee.

Robert Garioch

Amorous Greetings
(in terms of the essential)

When all is told
in whatever words,

it's each other
that our arms enfold.

Gael Turnbull

Brian Johnstone

Sonnet (XLVI)

Of the stars I admired, drenched
by different rivers and dews,
I only chose the one I loved
and since then I sleep with the night.

Of the waves, one wave and another wave,
green sea, green cold, green branch,
I only chose a single wave:
the invisible wave of your body.

All the drops, all the roots,
all the threads of light came,
they came to see me sooner or later.

I wanted your head of hair to myself.
And of all the gifts of my country
I only chose your wild heart.

Pablo Neruda   translated by John Manson

Pomegranate

(for Jean)

on my table
            the matrix
of a fruit
                        no less
for having failed to grow

pomegranate
            apple of love
your rusty sheen
                        glows
like a waning sun
            too late
to mature
            and fall
                        you set
in the bittersweet beauty
            of youth

opened
        your heart
                        to the spring
let your tears
                dry

Brian Johnstone

James McGonigal

Meng Chiao
    Impromptu
    translated by A. C. Graham

James McGonigal
    Eye Of The Beholder

Impromptu

Keep away from sharp swords,
Don't go near a lovely woman.
A sharp sword too close will wound your hand,
Woman's beauty too close will wound your life.
The danger of the road is not in the distance,
Ten yards is enough to break a wheel.
The peril of love is not in loving too often,
A single evening can leave its wound in the soul.

Meng Chiao (AD 751-814)   translated by A. C. Graham

The garden pool's eye glazes
in a dream of evaporation: help I'm expiring
fern stems and sun's lips sucking
my water-skin tighter

quick fill me with tears – bucketfuls
of the shocking drops between lashes of bulrush.
Everything clouds, clears; three goldfish
gleam in a pupil appraising the blue

and in their midst, with dripping basin, you.

James McGonigal

Iain Crichton Smith
  The World's a Minefield

kevin macneil
  Lloret de Mar

The World's A Minefield

The world's a minefield when I think of you.
I must walk carefully in case I touch
some irretrievable and secret switch
that blows the old world back into the new.

How careless I once was about this ground
with the negligence of ignorance. Now I take
the smallest delicate steps and now I look
about me and about me without end.

Iain Crichton Smith

Lloret de Mar

Each sunbeat slow-wings a scent of sun
lotion. Inner perfume of you.
The heaving ocean.

Back home, you will be sauntering
in tight, cold circles,
a first wedding ring.

I'm all laid out,
the sun darkening my sleep.
Ach, a ghaoil ghil, this was no break.

My hurt skin weeps.

kevin macneil
'Ach, a ghaoll ghil . . ' (Gaelic) (Vocative) 'But, my white love . . .'

Richard Price

The Gallant Weaver

Where Cart rins rowin to the sea
By mony a flow'r and spreading tree,
There lives a lad, the lad for me –
    He is a gallant weaver.
O' I had wooers aught or nine,
They gied me rings and ribbons fine,
And I was fear'd my heart wad tine,
    And I gied it to the weaver.

My daddie sign'd my tocher-band
To gie the lad that has the land;
But to my heart I'll add my hand,
    And give it to the weaver.
While birds rejoice in leafy bowers,
While bees delight in opening flowers,
While corn grows green in summer showers,
    I love my gallant weaver.

Robert Burns

John Gallagher

Speak to me again, John Gallagher
at work if no the house.
Ah've took up ma hem for you,
skooshed scent in ma blouse.

Ma says you're a boy fae the Port,
a druggie and no all there.
She minds yer 'sensitive hands'
were fists at the Kilma fair.

Come to the shop, John Gallagher,
meet me on ma break.
If you're no a Prudential man
that's a risk Ah'll have to take.

Richard Price

Iain S. Mac a' Phearsain

Iain Mac a' Ghobhainn/Iain Crichton Smith
    Tha Thu Air Aigeann M' Inntinn/
    You Are At The Bottom Of My Mind

Iain S. Mac a' Phearsain/John S. MacPherson
    Air Bhog/Launched

Tha Thu Air Aigeann M' Inntinn

Gun fhios dhomh tha thu air aigeann m' inntinn
mar fhear-tadhail grunnd na mara
le chlogaid 's a dhà shùil mhòir
's chan aithne dhomh ceart d' fhiamh no do dhòigh
an dèidh còig bliadhna shiantan
tìme dòrtadh eadar mise 's tù:

beanntan bùirn gun ainm a' dòrtadh
eadar mise 'gad shlaodadh air bòrd
's d' fhiamh 's do dhòighean 'nam làmhan fann.
Chaidh thu air chall
am measg lusan dìomhair a' ghrunnda
anns an leth-sholas uaine gun ghràdh,

's chan èirich thu chaoidh air bhàrr cuain
a chaoidh 's mo làmhan a' slaodadh gun sgur
's chan aithne dhomh do shlighe idir,
thus' ann an leth-sholas do shuain
a' tathaich aigeann na mara gun tàmh
's mise slaodadh 's a' slaodadh air uachdar cuain.

Iain Mac a' Ghobhainn

You Are At The Bottom Of My Mind

Without my knowing it you are at the bottom of my mind
like a visitor to the bottom of the sea
with his helmet and his two large eyes
and I do not rightly know your appearance or your manner
after five years of showers
of time pouring between me and you:

nameless mountains of water pouring
between me hauling you on board
and your appearance and manner in my weak hands.
You went astray
among the mysterious plants of the sea-bed
in the green half-light without love,

 and you will never rise to the surface
though my hands are hauling ceaselessly
and I do not know your way at all,
you in the half-light of your sleep
haunting the bed of the sea without ceasing
and I hauling and hauling on the surface.

Iain Crichton Smith

Air Bhog

gam chur air bhog
air feasgar foghair
an cuan is am bus air
’s an t-uisge a’ breith air na siùil

agus thusa air chruaidh
air do cheangal
nad aodann siar
nad chorragan sèimh
a’ fosgladh neòil na maidne

’s ar cùrsa dìreach bho seo a-mach
eadar dà acarsaid
a’ cumail ron ghaoith
a dh’ionnsaigh fàire
freagairt buain

Iain S. Mac a' Phearsain

Launched

launching myself
on an autumn afternoon
the sea pouting
the rain grabbing at the sails

and you docked
tied up
in your westcoast face
in your fine fingers
opening morning clouds

and our course from here on in
between two harbours
before the wind
toward the horizon
of one never-ending answer

John S. MacPherson

Roddy Lumsden

Poem for a Goodbye

When you go through
My absence, which is all of you,
And clouds, or suns, no more can be my sky,
My one dissembling will be all –
The inclusive lie
Of being this voice, this look, these few feet tall.

The elements which
Made me from our encounter rich
Cannot be uncreated; there is no
Chaos whose informality
Can cancel so
The ritual of your presence, even gone away.

You, then, and I
Will masquerade a lie,
Diminishing ourselves to be what can
Seem one without the other, while
A greater man,
In hiding, lies behind this look, this smile.

It's he who will
Across sad oceans meet you still,
Startling your carelessness with what once was.
His voice from this past hour will speak,
Cancelling Time's laws:
In the world's presence his hand will touch your cheek.

Foreign can be
Only that sound to you and me.
There is no thought that in its dying goes
Through such a region we do not
In it compose
Each other's selves, each in the other's thought.

You leave behind
More than I was, and with a kind
Of sad prevarication take with you
More than I'll be till that day when
Nothing's to do
But say, 'At last', and we are home again.

Norman MacCaig

Halfway Across

A week I waited for the call from you.
Now two desk-drumming hours have lapsed, I think
Less of the minutes we were interlinked
Than of those giddy moments halfway through
We spent cut off, when I stood in the hall
And knew the wire dead beneath my feet
Like Blondin crossing the Niagra Falls
Blindfolded, waiting for a breeze to shift,
For balance to indulge me, you to lift
The set and, bidding, opt for Call Repeat
To ring the silence down. I steadied, knelt
To take the thrill of it, the intimate
Exchange you gift me into and I felt
A pulse; a ripple in the infinite.

Roddy Lumsden

Tom Pow

Pablo Neruda
   Your Breast Is Enough
   translated by W. S. Merwin

Tom Pow
   Island Love

Your Breast Is Enough

Your breast is enough for my heart,
and my wings for your freedom.
What was sleeping above your soul will rise
out of my mouth to heaven.

In you is the illusion of each day.
You arrive like the dew to the cupped flowers.
You undermine the horizon with your absence.
Eternally in flight like the wave.

I have said that you sang in the wind
like the pines and like the masts.
Like them you are tall and taciturn,
and you are sad, all at once, like a voyage.

You gather things to you like an old road.
You are peopled with echoes and nostalgic voices.
I awoke and at times birds fled and migrated
that had been sleeping in your soul.

Pablo Neruda   translated by W. S. Merwin

Island Love

You walk up from the strand, your creel brimming
with herring; you come down from the hill,
your creel laden with turf, your grey-green eyes
cast down on the stony path, your black hair

wet with sweat or a moil of salty mist;
and glad am I there's a bond between us
for it seems to me I'm a poor catch
for this world. My fishing lines tangle and break

in calm waters, lobsters climb from my pots
to go seeking greater challenge elsewhere;
when the sea heaves and gurls back, I'm the first
to lose hope. I set sail with hymns on my lips.

Others there are that would have built for you
a better house; stones that knitted tightly
against the bitter wind, capped with a roof
the hens couldn't lay in. Such men would have turf

stacked for ten winters and then turf to spare;
men to make you proud their knowledge was sought,
their courage praised: for did they not leap
Bull's Cove for you, from black rock to black rock,

as down below fulmars wheeled and the white
water thundered in? They did? God bless them!
But you have a dreamer, a grim fisher
in melancholy; an idler who stares
into the tell-tale smoor of the fire, his tale
often the heaviest creel you carry.
Feckless, your father called me, indolent,
your mother: our tongue is rich in name-tags.

Your love is a mystery and a blessing.
No matter where the black dogs take me,
towards overhang or scree, you guide me
back to clear tracks of sunlight; constantly

giving our lives the shape of the journey
they are on. You make plans for the market
and provision for each birth. You let faith
take care of the rest – a deep faith that shines

in those bright grey-green eyes, a faith that sees
the lines of my life when I do not,
that welcomes me dripping from the dark sea
when we give up our tired white bodies with joy.

Tom Pow

Meg Bateman

Robert Burns
 Ae Fond Kiss

Meg Bateman
 Pòg/Kiss

Ae Fond Kiss

Ae fond kiss, and then we sever;
Ae farewell and then for ever!
Deep in heart-wrung tears I'll pledge thee,
Warring sighs and groans I'll wage thee.

Who shall say that fortunes grieves him
While the star of hope she leaves him?
Me, nae chearful twinkle lights me;
Dark despair around benights me.

I'll ne'er blame my partial fancy,
Naething could resist my Nancy:
but to see her, was to love her;
Love but her, and love for ever.

Had we never lov'd sae kindly,
Had we never lov'd sae blindly,
Never met – or never parted,
We had ne'er been broken-hearted.

Fare thee weel, thou first and fairest!
Fare thee weel, thou best and dearest!
Thine be ilka joy and treasure,
Peace, Enjoyment, Love, and Pleasure!

Ae fond kiss, and then we sever!
Ae fareweel, Alas, for ever!
Deep in heart-wrung tears I'll pledge thee,
Warring sighs and groans I'll wage thee.

Robert Burns

Pòg

Ar ciad phòg na pòig-dhealachaidh
is m' inntinn ga luasgadh fad an fheasgair
le blàths do bhilean,
mo chridhe ga lìonadh uair eile
le iargain gun fheum, is eadarainn
an Cuan Sgìth is fichead bliadhna
is mi a' strì ri m' ùidh a tharraing
gu sgioblachadh dhèideagan
a' strì rì m' ùidh ortsa
thionndadh gu ùidh màthar.

Meg Bateman

Kiss

Our first kiss a kiss of parting,
and all evening my mind rocked
by the warmth of your lips,
my heart again swollen
by a useless longing, the Minch
and twenty years between us . . .
as I strive to turn my mind
to tidying up the toys,
strive to turn my desire
into the regard of a mother.

Meg Bateman

G. F. Dutton

No One So Much As You

No one so much as you
Loves this my clay,
Or would lament as you
Its dying day.

You know me through and through
Though I have not told,
And though with what you know
You are not bold.

None ever was so fair
As I thought you:
Not a word can I bear
Spoken against you.

All that ever I did
For you seemed coarse
Compared with what I hid
Nor put in force.

My eyes scarce dare meet you
Lest they should prove
I but respond to you
And do not love.

We look and understand,
We cannot speak
Except in trifles and
Words the most weak.

For I at most accept
Your love regretting
That is all: I have kept
Only a fretting

That I could not return
All that you gave
And could not ever burn
With the love you have,

Till sometimes it did seem
Better it were
Never to see you more
Than linger here

With only gratitude
Instead of love –
A pine in solitude
Cradling a dove.

Edward Thomas

Violets

violets are cruel, with pale
demanding scent,
wet grass displays its knives, birds
shriek argument

all is fresh and bitter as
an apple's core.
I put the new day by, go back
to you still there

standing at the gateside glad
the morning is so fine and glad
to see me on so fine a morning glad.

G. F. Dutton

Alan Riach

Of My First Love

O my first love! You are in my life forever
Like the Eas-Coul-aulin* in Sutherlandshire
Where the Amhainnan Loch Bhig burn
Plunges over the desolate slopes of Leitir Dubh.
Silhouetted against grim black rocks
This foaming mountain torrent
With its source in desolate tarns
Is savage in the extreme
As its waters with one wild leap
Hurl over the dizzy brink
Of the perpendicular cliff-face
In that great den of nature,
To be churned into spray
In the steaming depths below.
Near its base the fall splits up
Into cascades spreading out like a fan.
A legend tells how a beautiful maiden
In desperation threw herself
Over the cataract – the waters
Immediately took on the shape
Of her waving hair,
And on moonlight nights she is still to be seen
Lying near the base of the fall
Gazing up at the tremendous cascade
Of some six-hundred feet!

O my first love! Even you so lie
Near the base of my precipitous, ever lonelier and colder life
With your fair hair still rippling out
As I remember it between my fingers
When you let me unloosen first
(Over thirty chaotic years ago!)
That golden tumult forever!

Hugh MacDiarmid

*The beautiful Fall of Coul – the highest waterfall in Scotland – its name meaning, in Gaelic, tresses of hair.

Of Love

There's an old film called The Minister's Wife *where Cary Grant plays an angel come to earth to work a few miracles. One shot reveals him, hands clasped behind his back, his back to a table with an almost empty bottle of wine on it. Another drink is called for. Unobserved, his index finger points to the low meniscus, runs up the side of the bottle, and the content refills, by magic. Love works unobtrusively, like that.*

If I could bring them all together,
what would I have?

An image of her, smiling in excitement,
approaching in the crowd on London Bridge.

An image of her, thoughtful in her yellow dress,
walking down the grey slope of the street.

And an image of her, at nightfall, hand in hand with me,
crossing the field to a tryst, with kindling fire inside.

And of her, under the tree, laughter light as a bird's wings,
her face, her hands strong as branches.

And of her, standing in the doorway bidding me goodbye.
And of her again, standing in the doorway, returned at last forever.

If I put them all together now, in twenty-seven years,
and called to the ends of the earth, all exultations, fears,

and no predictions count, yet I would say
with certainty: There was love. Now, let it stay.

Alan Riach

Alexander Hutchison

Alexander Montgomerie
Evin Deid Behold I Breathe

Alexander Hutchison
Hole House Farm

Evin Deid Behold I Breathe

Evin deid behold I breathe!
    My breath procures my pane;
Els dolour eftir death,
    Sould slaik when I war slane:
    Bot destinie's disdane
So span my fatall threid,
    Bot* mercy to remane
A martyr quick and deid.
    O cruell deidly feid!
    O rigour but remorse!
Since thair is no remeid,
    Come patience perforce.

Yit tyme sall try my treuth
    And panefull patient pairt,
Tho' love suld rage but reuth
    And death with deidly dairt
    Suld sey to caus me smairt,
Nor fortun's fickill wheill:
    All suld not change my hairt
Whilk is als true as steill.
I am not lyk ane eill
    To slippe away and slyde.
Love, fortun, death, fairweill
    For I am bound to byde.

Alexander Montgomerie

*The first use of 'bot' is certainly *but,* and perhaps something of it in the second,
but for the rest it means *without.*

Hole House Farm

The children have
got a bonfire going
in the back garden

4 potatoes 3 eggs
and next to no idea
of how to go about it.

Three sheep
with long tails
in the middle distance
crunch their way
towards me.

Rain spots down;
the evening cools
to grey and green.

* * *

If I were to say
to you my heart is
like a log on fire

it wouldn't be true
not even close

but the nearest
thing I have to love is
this – is you – here
even when
the desperate animals

interrupt and some
dog makes the mistake
of barking all
strangers away.

Alexander Hutchison

Valerie Gillies

The guidman of Crandart
from Oran le Fear Chrannard an Gleann Ìle / Glen Isla Love Song
rendered by Valerie Gillies

Valerie Gillies
The Space Between Us

Oran le Fear Chrannard an Gleann Ìle

'S mòr mo mhulad 's cha lugh' m' èislein,
  ge b' è dh' èisteadh rium;

's tric mi 'g amharc thar a' bhealach,
  's m' air' air dol a-nunn.

(Verses 1 and 2)

Glen Isla Love Song

My longing wastes me with its yearning,
  Whoever will listen to me, hear

How often I'm looking up at the high pass
  With my mind on travelling over Monega!

Late at night I'm longing to go
  To that glen on the far side

Where the blue-eyed girl will be,
  The shapely one with the long blonde hair.

Through the great pineforest on a pitchblack night
  I'd go, under a downpour of heavy rain.

I'd swim across without oar, without oak,
  If my love were on the other shore.

The river headlong in spate cannot hold me back
  Even if my stepping-stone goes under the wave.

I'll give that girl there a lovely shirt
  With silk at the cuffs of the sleeves,

And she'll give me a patterned crossbelt
  Richly diced and studded with silver.

Love overwhelms me for the girl by the Mar fir,
  The girl with the level gaze.

* * *

I'll be in misery if you're going to marry another
  While I'm kept up country among the bens.

No gap in my teeth, not a wrinkle on my face,
  There's never a wheeze in my chest;

You won't give me up for any weakness
  But for the sharp company of the lowlanders.

I don't know much about sowing barley
  Yet I'll provide young goats for you,

You'll get a stag from the high slope, a trout from the pool,
  And the antlered roebuck of the cairns,

The brindled mallard, the greylag of the western isles,
  And the swan of most elegant swimming,

A red bird of the dark moors, the grey hen's whitebelt son,
    And the handsome steed of the wood, the capercaillie.

If I owned everything as far as Lochaber
    And even further beyond, with maybe

Elgin o' Moray and Edinburgh along with it
    And all the lands in between,

They'd count for nothing, I'd reject them all
    Before I would give up our pledge.

The guidman of Crandart   rendered by Valerie Gillies

The Space Between Us

In his glen one song always goes on air
Round the lip of Corrie Vanoch where I first heard it.
I see him everywhere I look, a moving figure,
Spring-heeled he walks the slopes, leaps the stream,
And he speaks from the well-head of Tobar a Chinn.

When I follow the pass up towards Monega,
Time is running by me with a sleety kiss
And a footprint appears in new snow beside mine.
If I turn round suddenly in the fields of his farm
His gaunt good looks are easily seen on Craig Soilleur.

Over the high ridge of Cuingard I hear the storm
Eddy through cliff and cleft like a windpipe,
While his song keeps on coming, a torrent
That never stops flowing through the ravine.
The space between us takes shape where he calls
On love, in the breezeway of Glen Isla's sonic seam.

Valerie Gillies

Hamish Henderson

Ewan MacColl
  The Joy Of Living

Hamish Henderson
  Vivamus Mea Lesbia Atque Amemus

The Joy of Living

Farewell you Northern hills, you mountains all, goodbye;
Moorland and stony ridges, crags and peaks, goodbye.
Glyder Fach farewell, Cul Beig, Scafell, cloud-bearing Suilven.
Sun-warmed rock and the cold of Bleaklow's frozen sea –
The snow and the wind and the rain on hills and mountains.
Days in the sun and the tempered wind and the air like wine,
And you drink and you drink till you're drunk on the joy of living.

Farewell to you, my love, my time is almost done.
Lie in my arms once more until the darkness comes.
You filled all my days, held the night at bay, dearest companion.
Years pass by and are gone with the speed of birds in flight,
Our life like the verse of a song heard in the mountains.
Give me your hand then, love, and join your voice with mine,
We'll sing of the hurt and the pain and the joy of living.

Farewell to you, my chicks, soon you must fly alone,
Flesh of my flesh, my future life, bone of my bone.
May your wings be strong, may your days be long, safe be your journey.
Each of you bears inside of you the gift of love,
May it bring you light and warmth and the pleasure of giving;
Eagerly savour each new day and the taste of its mouth,
Never lose sight of the thrill and the joy of living.

Take me to some high place of heather, rock and ling,
Scatter my dust and ashes, feed me to the wind,
So that I will be part of all you see, the air you are breathing –
I'll be part of the curlew's cry and the soaring hawk,
The blue milkwort and the sundew hung with diamonds;
I'll be riding the gentle wind that blows through your hair,
Reminding you how we shared in the joy of living.

Ewan MacColl

Vivamus Mea Lesbia Atque Amemus

for Gayle, on her birthday

Noo Gayle, my dear, ye maunna fear
    The snash o' dour auld bodies O.
It's daft to miss a single kiss
    Tae please sic muckle cuddies O.

Live while ye may, and lo'e the day –
    In life there's naething certain O.
Oor peerie licht sune ends in nicht,
    When Fate rings doon the curtain O.

Sae kiss me mair – and mair – and mair:
    A thoosan kisses gie me O.
– But dinna count the haill amount
    Lest a' my senses lea me O.

Hamish Henderson
after Catullus

Walter Perrie

Ode à Cassandre

Mignonne, allon voir si la rose
Qui ce matin auoit declose
Sa robe de pourpre, au soleil,
A point perdu cette vesprée,
Les plis de sa robe pourprée
Et son teint au vostre pareil.

    Las, voiés comme en peu d'espace,
Mignonne, elle a dessus la place
Las, las, ses beautés laissé cheoir!
O vraiment maratre Nature,
Puis qu'une telle fleur ne dure
Que du matin iusques au soir.

    Donc, si vous me croiés, mignonne:
Tandis que vôtre age fleuronne
En sa plus verte nouveauté:
Cueillés, cueillés vôtre ieunesse,
Comme a cette fleur, la viellesse
Fera ternir vôtre beauté.

Pierre de Ronsard (1553)

The Riddle

In sighs and embraces
embraces and kisses
all our love passes
passes away.

Having you
between my arms
a breathing form
breathless, warm
for a day, a night
night and a day
is having
eternity.

In day and night
night and a day
all our time passes
passes away.

Walter Perrie

Peter McCarey

Robert Henryson
    from The Testament of Cresseid

Peter McCarey
    from 'Tantris'

from The Testament of Cresseid

This royall ring set with this rubie reid
Quhilk Troylus in dowrie to me send,
To him agane I leif it quhen I am deid
To mak my cairfull deid unto him kend:
Thus I conclude schortlie, and mak ane end:
My spreit I leif to Diane quhair scho dwellis,
To walk with hir in waist woddis and wellis.

'O Diomeid, thou hes baith broche and belt
Quhilk Troylus gave me in takning
Of his trew lufe!' And with that word scho swelt.
And sone ane lipper man tuik of the ring,
Syne buryit hir withouttin tarying.
To Troylus furthwith the ring he bair
And of Cresseid the deith he can declair.

Quhen he had hard hir greit infirmitie,
Hir legacie and lamentatioun,
And how scho endit in sic povertie,
He swelt for wo and fell doun in ane swoun;
For greit sorrow his hart to brist was boun:
Siching full sadlie said: 'I can no moir –
Scho was untrew and wo is me thairfoir.'

Sum said he maid ane tomb of merbell gray,
And wrait hir name and superscriptioun,
And laid it on hir grave quhair that scho lay,
In goldin letteris, conteining this ressoun:
'Lo, fair laydis! Cresseid of Troyis toun,
Sumtyme countit the flour of womanheid,
Under this stane, lait lipper, lyis deid.'

Now, worthie wemen, in this ballet schort,
Maid for your worschip and instructioun;
Of cheritie, I monische and exhort:
Ming not your lufe with fals deceptioun.
Beir in your mynd this schort conclusioun
Of fair Cresseid – as I have said befoir;
Sen scho is deid, I speik of hir no moir.

Robert Henryson

162

'Tantris' (III)

Don't go. Don't let the morning
turn your head with her shivering, thin grace,
in silk like a tarn that just forgot the starlight
before the sun takes its usual way with her.
    If dawn were a dove on the window ledge . . .
    but you don't want to know.

Don't go – all this in the dark, her lying there
like moonlight on the bed, like a memory,
beyond recall already, now the blackbirds
were telling the town what we had done that night,
    carving our initials
    on each other's hearts. They sang

Don't go – but the night was parcelled up in binbags.
You're on my mind so much, I hardly know
the noonday sun or frost in the bones of morning
and holy Joe the horseman telling folk
    he'd strip me bare as innocence
    and lead me back to the light

(relax, he'll never know I've let you in here);
the only man I ever hured with was him.
Goodbye: the yellow planets and the grey
dawn will attend you on your way. The sun
    will get around this blind. The sun
    will lever us apart.

I have her crouching at this square of canvas
quite naked. Black canvas. Black on white.
Heavy hair pinned up, and chin to cheekbone
mulled in light, like a pebble in the hand.
    She pulls the black aside –
    she rolls it up, we disappear.

Peter McCarey

David Kinloch

Hart Crane
   The Harbor Dawn

David Kinloch
   Bed

The Harbor Dawn

Insistently through sleep – a tide of voices –
They meet you listening midway in your dream,
The long, tired sounds, fog-insulated noises:
Gongs in white surplices, beshrouded wails,
Far strum of fog horns . . . signals dispersed in veils.

And then a truck will lumber past the wharves
As winch engines begin throbbing on some deck;
Or a drunken stevedore's howl and thud below
Comes echoing alley-upward through dim snow.

And if they take your sleep away sometimes
They give it back again. Soft sleeves of sound
Attend the darkling harbor, the pillowed bay;
Somewhere out there in blankness steam

Spills into steam, and wanders, washed away
– Flurried by keen fifings, eddied
Among distant chiming buoys – adrift. The sky,

Cool feathery fold, suspends, distills
This wavering slumber . . . Slowly –
Immemorially the window, the half-covered chair
Ask nothing but this sheath of pallid air.

And you beside me, blessèd now while sirens
Sing to us, stealthily weave us into day –
Serenely now, before day claims our eyes
Your cool arms murmurously about me lay.

While myriad snowy hands are clustering at the panes –

    your hands within my hands are deeds;
    my tongue upon your throat – singing
    arms close; eyes wide, undoubtful
            dark
                drink the dawn –
    a forest shudders in your hair!

The window goes blond slowly. Frostily clears.
From Cyclopean towers across Manhattan waters
– Two – three bright window-eyes aglitter, disk
The sun, released – aloft with cold gulls hither.

The fog leans one last moment on the sill.
Under the mistletoe of dreams, a star –
As though to join us at some distant hill –
Turns in the waking west and goes to sleep.

Hart Crane

Bed

The moment the light goes out,
He sleeps: a gift from the dark.
There is the small chime
Of the moon on the wall,
The deep freeze digesting
In the kitchen. He floats
From head to toe on the buzz
Of his snore, dreaming the calm
Glide of a Jasper ski-lift,
The summer elk that trotted
Out of forest beneath our
Dangling feet. His arm
Crooks the violin of my head.
I elbow him away intent on
Sleep but suddenly, unpegged
By a gust of dreams, we roll
Together in the hot hole
Of his mum's old bed,
Dribbling on the pillows.
Waking, he has me in an
Arm-lock, our legs a single
Rope of flesh, my ear-lobe
Tickled by his breath. I reach
Behind me and shove my hand
Between his thighs. He stretches,
Opening briefly like a centre –
Fold, a light smile of welcome
On his lips. But more than this
Is the scrape of the two-o' clock

Beetle, the nip of a dust-mite,
My scratch: my love disturbed
By me, awake but patient
In the dark.

David Kinloch

W. N. Herbert

Boris Pasternak
   To A Friend
   translated by Edwin Morgan

W. N. Herbert
   I Confess . . .

To A Friend

You think I don't know darkness must reach light?
You think I'm pleased to see these gleams rebuffed?
Only a monster would not prefer the delight
A million win, if an idle hundred are sloughed.

I too am measured by the five year plan.
I fall and rise as that plan draws its breath.
Only – what is it that the breastbone of a man
Conceals? What slows me like the sloth of death?

Great soviets have still one stumbling-block.
High places for high passions must be set.
The poet's place is vacant, is it not?
If it is not, look to your soviet.

Boris Pasternak   translated by Edwin Morgan

I Confess . . .

I would inform on you
if the two of us were
in the middle of a terror:
I'd tell them what they'd think you'd do.

I'd let them into our flat
our reading sleeping writing room,
you'd go to God knows what
not knowing who to blame.

All our friends would board
the smallest of trains
for the fastest of journeys
through their threatening brains.

I tell you this my dear
in the gentlest of times
since other souls elsewhere
must pay for my crimes.

W. N. Herbert

Kate Clanchy

•

A Lecture Upon The Shadow

Stand still, and I will read to thee
A Lecture, love, in Loves philosophy.
        These three houres that we have spent,
        Walking here, Two shadowes went
Along with us, which we our selves produc'd;
But, now the Sunne is just above our head,
        We doe those shadowes tread;
        And to brave clearnesse all things are reduc'd.
    So whilst our infant loves did grow,
    Disguises did, and shadowes, flow,
    From us, and our cares; but, now 'tis not so.

That love hath not attain'd the high'st degree,
Which is still diligent lest others see.

Except our loves at this noone stay,
We shall new shadowes make the other way.
        As the first were made to blinde
        Others; these which come behinde
Will worke upon our selves, and blind our eyes.
If our loves faint, and westwardly decline;
        To me thou, falsly, thine,
        And I to thee mine actions shall disguise.
    The morning shadowes weare away,
    But these grow longer all the day,
    But oh, loves day is short, if love decay.

Love is a growing, or full constant light;
And his first minute, after noone, is night.

John Donne

Heliograph

(after 'A Lecture Upon The Shadow')

This, my love, if we believe John Donne,
is the best we'll get, love's brief high noon –
      it seems we've just walked out
      blinking, pallid, ill-equipped,
sans sun cream, phrase book, hat
into a marble mezzogiorno square
      after years in a damp cloister.
      We tread the burning ground like cats,
   crush short shadows underfoot –
   I've never been much good with heat.
   I shake, and turn to you, and stick

nuzzling for scrap of shade. From here
you're statuesque, but bleared –

there's too much sun. Hold me close –
and straight, we're here to pose
      for a photograph, a portrait
      on self-timer. We'll look like tourists,
I expect: crumpled, modern, lost
holding up incongruous thumbs
      under faces shadowed deep as skulls –
      hopelessly small and un-baroque.
   It's hard to smile in direct light.
   Let's shut our eyes, count down the ticks
   and when we open at the click, squint

and see, beyond the square, a gap of shade –
an arch, an opening, a colonnade of days.

Kate Clanchy

Don Paterson

Antonio Machado
  Los Ojos

Don Paterson
  The Eyes

Los Ojos

I

Cuando murió su amada
pensó en hacerse viejo
en la mansión cerrada,
solo, con su memoria y el espejo
donde ella se miraba un claro dia.
Como el oro en el arca del avaro,
pensó que no guardaría
todo un ayer en el espejo claro.
Ya el tiempo para el no correría.

II

Mas, pasado el primer aniversario,
¿ cómo eran – preguntó – pardos o negros,
¿ sus ojos? ¿Glaucos? . . . ¿Grises?
¿ Como eran, ¡Santo Dios!, que no recuerdo? . . .

III

Salió a la calle un día
de primavera, y paseó en silencio
su doble luto, el corazon cerrado . . .
De una ventana en el sombrió hueco
vio unos ojos brillar. Bajó los suyos
y suigió su camino . . . ¡Como esos!

Antonio Machado

The Eyes

I

When his beloved died
he decided to grow old
and shut himself inside
the empty house, alone
with his memories of her
and the big sunny mirror
where she'd fixed her hair.
This great block of gold
he hoarded like a miser,
thinking here, at least,
he'd lock away the past,
keep one thing intact.

II

But around the first anniversary,
he began to wonder, to his horror,
about her eyes: Were they brown or black,
or grey? Green? Christ! I can't say . . .

III

One Spring morning, something gave in him;
shouldering his twin grief like a cross,
he shut the front door, turned into the street
and had walked just ten yards, when, from a dark close,
he caught a flash of eyes. He lowered his hat-brim
and walked on . . . yes, they were like that; like that . . .

Don Paterson

John Burnside

The Deer

What the deer at night consume
may be what we thought we needed
but can live without.

Try to forget your labor, the hours
you dug out the grove of young walnuts
to fill the neglected arbor with sun –

the vines like someone's handwriting
gone haywire with age,
wandering outside the lines.

Watching as you re-strung
what was left years ago to die,
I doubted anything could bloom,

but soon enough, tendrils, leaves,
then pea-sized grapes bubbled up,
chameleon-green clusters.

And as quickly as one can read
into the smallest gesture
the future, we conjured the mussel-blue

Concord – then, just as fast,
because the past is nobody's fool,
the sweet skin of someone gone.

We each have our own aftertaste
(in the vines, the bees tracing figure eights),
what our years of plenty rub up:

a flurry of talcum, a scented wrist.
Then (worse?) – remembering how to shine
the grape as if wiping a film of dust

from a frame – a picture
of what was once. The vintage.
And those who tended us.

And the deer, what memories
lodged in their bodies,
what hunger, as they helped themselves

to our unripe fruit? Under the poor lantern
of the moon, stealthy ghosts,
they stripped the grapes

as we slept, dreaming as always
our versions of Pharoah's dream.
We could grieve awake,

but given the liquid passage of the animal
through the dark, a current,
like it or not, we can't stop,

we go out after dinner to watch
the doe and her young feed on our apples.
Beautiful thieves, in the falling light

the color of grain
the wise store inside
after the growing season is over.

Allison Funk

Animals

There are nights when we cannot name
the animals that flit across our headlights,

even on moonlit journeys, when the road
is eerie and still

and we smell the water long before
the coast road, or those lamps across the bay,

they cross our path, unnameable and bright
as any in the sudden heat of Eden.

Mostly, it's rabbit, or fox, though we've sometimes caught
a glimpse of powder blue, or Chinese white,

or chanced upon a mystery of eyes
and passed the last few miles in wonderment.

It's like the time our only neighbour died
on Echo Road,

leaving her house unoccupied for months,
a darkness at the far end of the track

that set itself apart,
the empty stairwell brooding in the heat,

the blank rooms filling with scats
and the dreams of mice.

In time, we came to think that house contained
a presence: we could see it from the yard

shifting from room to room in the autumn rain
and we thought it was watching us: a kindred shape

more animal than ghost.
They say, if you dream an animal, it means

'the self' – that mess of memory and fear
that wants, remembers, understands, denies,

and even now, we sometimes wake from dreams
of moving from room to room, with its scent on our hands

and a slickness of musk and fur
on our sleep-washed skins,

yet what I sense in this, and cannot tell
is not the continuity we understand

as self, but life, beyond the life we live
on purpose: one broad presence that proceeds

by craft and guesswork,
shadowing our love.

John Burnside

Author Notes

Meg Bateman

Meg Bateman was born in 1959 in Edinburgh. She teaches at Sabhal Mor Ostaig in Skye. Her collections are *Orain Ghaoil*, (Coisceim, 1991), *Aotromachd/Lightness* (Polygon, 1997) and *Estruscan Reader IX* (Estruscan Books, 1998).

John Burnside

John Burnside has published seven books of poems, of which the most recent is *The Asylum Dance*, (Jonathan Cape, 2000), two novels, *The Dumb House* and *The Mercy Boys*, and a book of short stories, *Burning Elvis*, (Jonathan Cape, 2000). Allison Funk has published two books of poetry, *Forms of Conversion* and *Living at the Epicentre*. She teaches at Southern Illinois University.

Kate Clanchy

Kate Clanchy's most recent collection is *Samarkand* (Picador, 1999).

Thomas A. Clark

Thomas A. Clark runs the Cairn Gallery in Nailsworth, Gloucestershire with Laurie Clark. His poetry is gathered in *Tormentil & Bleached Bones* (Polygon, 1993) and numerous publications from Moschatel Press.

'Robert Creeley is the poet of our time who has pushed the "love poem" beyond praise or petition to a sustained, troubled intimacy which opens the poem to daily, often momentary, negotiations between self and other, the crushing or liberating distances and impingements.'

Ken Cockburn

Ken Cockburn was born in Kirkcaldy in 1960. He works with the Scottish Poetry Library. *Souvenirs and Homelands*, his first collection of poems, was published by Scottish Cultural Press (1998).

'These poems were written during Goethe's second visit to Italy in 1790. The first visit, four years earlier, had been a seminal event in his life, when he had discovered the reality of the classical world and physical love. The second also had its pleasures, but there is a worldliness, even cynicism, in many poems.'

Stewart Conn

Stewart Conn's latest dramatic works include *Clay Bull* and a version of George Mackay Brown's novel *Greenvoe*. A volume of his selected poems *Stolen Light* (Bloodaxe) was launched at the 1998 Edinburgh Book Festival. Alicia Spottiswoode (Lady John Scott) was born in 1810 and died in 1900, forty years a widow. A staunch Jacobite, a keen conservationist and an early collector of folk music, her reputation as a composer rests primarily on her version of 'Annie Laurie'.

Robert Crawford

Robert Crawford was born in Bellshill in 1959. He is Professor of Modern Scottish Literature at the University of St Andrews. His collections include *Masculinity* (Jonathan Cape, 1996) and *Spirit Machines* (Jonathan Cape, 1999). He co-edited *The Penguin Book of Poetry from Britain and Ireland since 1945* (1998) and *The New Penguin Book of Scottish Verse* (2000). Marion Angus (1866-1946) came from Arbroath where she was a daughter of the manse. Her *Selected Poems* were published in 1950.

Christine De Luca

Christine De Luca is from Shetland and lives in Edinburgh. She writes in English and Shetlandic and has two collections, *Voes & Sounds* (1995) and *Wast wi da Valkyries* (1997, Shetland Library).

Colin Donati

Colin Donati is a widely anthologised poet and musician. He currently lives in Edinburgh. Alexander Montgomerie (c.1550-1598) was the 'maistre poete' in the reign James VI. Love, treated with great variety of emotional and philosophical approach, is one of his major themes. Some intrigue attaches to his career in James' service and he was later excluded from the court.

G. F. Dutton

G. F. Dutton's *Selected Poems* will be published by Bloodaxe in 2000.

'Edward Thomas's is not a poem about his love, but about his wife Helen's love for him, and his incapacity to return it. It's a careful, clinical distinction between Love and Gratitude. It has always fascinated me, as has much of what this deeply split man wrote, for its dolicate, heartbreaking craftsmanship of dissection.'

Ian Hamilton Finlay

Ian Hamilton Finlay was born in Nassau, Bahamas, in 1925. Artist, poet and gardener, he has published over 1,000 books, cards and poem prints under the Wild Hawthorn Press imprint. The garden he created at Little Sparta is open to the public every Summer. In the 1960s he edited a poetry magazine, *Poor.Old.Tired.Horse*, named after a poem by his friend Robert Creeley.

Valerie Gillies

Valerie Gillies' publications include *Each Bright Eye, Bed of Stone, Tweed Journey, The Chanter's Tune* (all Canongate) and *The Ringing Rock*. She recently collaborated on an artist's book with Will Maclean, *St Kilda Waulking Song* (Morning Star). Prof. W. J. Watson, who included the song in his anthology *Bardachd Ghaidhlig*, relates that Robertson of Crandart 'was said to be a particularly strong and handsome man. He took part in the Forty-five, and is said to have supported the Prince when he was tired on the march south from Edinburgh.'

John Glenday

John Glenday works as a drugs counsellor in Dundee. His collections of poems include *The Apple Ghost* and *Undark* (Peterloo Poets, 1995). He has also edited *La Comete D'Halcyon*, a bilingual anthology of contemporary Scottish poetry (Belgium, 1998). William Soutar was born in 1898, and died an invalid in 1943, bedridden with chronic spondylitis for the last fourteen years of his life. He wrote in both Scots and English, writing his Scots poetry in the Perth dialect he had spoken and loved all his life.

Rody Gorman

Rody Gorman was born in Dublin in 1960 and moved to Skye in 1987 to learn Scottish Gaelic. He began writing verse in 1994. He teaches at the Gaelic college, Sabhal mor Ostaig.

Andrew Greig

Andrew Greig was born in Bannockburn and lives in Orkney and the Lothians. He has published poetry, novels and mountaineering expedition books. His collections of poems include *The Order of the Day* (Bloodaxe, 1990) and *Western Swing* (Bloodaxe, 1994).

Hamish Henderson

Hamish Henderson was born on Armistice day 1919. His Essays, *Alias MacAlias* (1992) and Letters, *The Armstrong Nose* (1996) are published by Polygon. Along with Ewan MacColl he helped shape the Scottish folk-song revival. This free rendering of Catullus is taken from a long poem sequence, 'Auld Reekie's Roses', as yet unfinished. Ewan MacColl was born in Salford, Lancashire, to Scots parents. He was an actor, playwright, folksinger and songwriter. This is one of the last songs he wrote, and can be found on *Black and White* (Cooking Vinyl CD 038). *The Essential Ewan MacColl Song Book* will be available from Music Sales in Spring 2000.

W. N. Herbert

W. N. Herbert's latest collection is *The Laurelude*, (Bloodaxe, 1999).

Tracey Herd

Tracey Herd was born in East Kilbride and is currently writer in residence at the University of Dundee. Her first book is *No Hiding Place* (Bloodaxe, 1996).

Matthew Hollis

Matthew Hollis was born in 1971 and graduated from Edinburgh University in 1996. He is co-editor of *Strong Words* (Bloodaxe, 2000) an anthology of poets on poetry.

Alexander Hutchison

Alexander Hutchison was born in Buckie on the Moray Firth coast. He currently lives in Glasgow. His collections are *Epitaph for a Butcher* (Akros, 1997) and the forthcoming *Scales Dog: Poems New and Selected*.

'I first heard this lyric of Montgomerie in a setting recorded by the Saltire Singers in 1974. The more-than-gloomy, measured, sometimes quickening tone owes much to the courtly, Petrarchan tradition.'

Robert Alan Jamieson

Born in Shetland, Robert Alan Jamieson is a novelist and poet, currently Writer in Residence at the universities of Glasgow and Strathclyde. His latest book is *Mount Hiddenabyss* in collaboration with the painter Graeme Todd, to be published by the Fruitmarket Gallery in spring 2000. George Campbell Hay's *Collected Poems* were published by W. L. Lorimer Trust and Polygon in 1999. This poem first appeared in *Fuaran Sleibb* (William MacLellan, 1947).

Brian Johnstone

Brian Johnstone was born in Edinburgh and now lives in Fife. His first full collection of poems was *The Lizard Silence* (Scottish Cultural Press, 1996). He was a founder of *Shore Poets*.

David Kinloch

David Kinloch was born in Glasgow in 1959. His poetry collections are *Dustie-Fute* (Vennel Press, 1992) and *Paris-Forfar* (Polygon, 1994); a selection of his work is published in *Dream State* (Polygon, 1994). He currently co-edits *Southfields*.

'The Harbor Dawn' is part of American poet Hart Crane's long poem 'The Bridge'. Published in 1930 it was only forty five years later that critics began to unravel the complex web of images expressing homosexual desire and love.'

Frank Kuppner

Frank Kuppner's most recent collection *Everything is Strange* was published by Carcanet. He is currently Writer in Residence at Edinburgh University. The translation of Sorley Maclean's love poem is by Iain Crichton Smith.

Tom Leonard

Tom Leonard was born in Glasgow in 1944. His poems are collected in *Intimate Voices* (Galloping Dog Press, 1984) and *Reports from the Present* (Jonathan Cape, 1995). He has a new selection in preparation.

'I chose "To Mary" because it's such a delicate and tender poem about what could easily have been mawkish or melodramatic – Cowper's fear of going under again to his depression mania when his companion Mary has already had a stroke. It's a practically minded poem about real love in old age and collapsing health.'

Roddy Lumsden

Roddy Lumsden's latest book of poems is *Yeah Yeah Yeah*, (Bloodaxe, 1997).

Peter McCarey

Peter McCarey's most recent collection of poetry is *Double-Click* (Akros, 1997). He works as a translator in Switzerland.

James McGonigal

James McGonigal is a teacher, editor and critic whose poetry has appeared in various anthologies and two collections *Unidentified Flying Poems* (1980) and *Driven Home* (1998). He is currently co-editing anthologies of Scottish religious poetry and Scots-Irish writing.

Anne Macleod

Anne Macleod lives on the Black Isle working as a dermatologist. Her collections of poems are *Standing by Thistles* (Scottish Cultural Press, 1997) and *Just the Caravaggio* (Poetry Salzburg, 1999). The translations of the Romanian poet and composer Nina Cassian are by Andrea Delatant and Brenda Walker.

aonghas macneacail

aonghas macneacail's most recent collection was a *Oideachadh Ceart/A Proper Schooling* (Polygon, 1998). He lives with his wife the actress Gerda Stevenson at Carlin's Loup in Carlops. 'The Fair Swan' is regarded as one of the most powerful Gaelic poems to come out of the First World War. Like other Gaelic poetry, it is usually sung, and remains one of the most popular songs in the Gaelic repertoire.

kevin macneil

kevin macneil was born and raised on the Isle of Lewis and is a widely published writer of poetry and prose, including *Love and Zen in the Outer Hebrides* (Canongate, 1998). He is currently Iain Crichton Smith writer in residence for the Highlands area, and lives on the Isle of Skye. He is editing a forthcoming pocketbooks anthology, *Wish I Was Here*.

John S. MacPherson

John S. MacPherson was born and raised on the Canadian prairie, of Skye and Islay descent. He is now a lecturer in Gaelic at Sabhal Mor Ostaig.

'I thought for years this poem was the most moving portrait of irreconcilable love, he or she above, the other below, lurking on the sea floor, the one pulling, the other sinking. It was only recently I was told the poet had written it about his brother, which doesn't alter my reaction a bit.'

Edwin Morgan

Edwin Morgan was born in Glasgow in 1920. He was appointed Poet Laureate of Glasgow in 1999. His books include *Collected Poems* (Carcanet, 1990), *Sweeping Out The Dark* (Carcanet 1994) and *Demon* (Mariscat, 1999) as well as the translation of *Cyrano de Bergerac* into Scots (Carcanet, 1992) and the revised *Doctor Faustus* (Canongate, 1999).

'Whatever sort of love the Dickinson poem celebrates, I love its sense of passionate abandon. Passion and fragmentariness link her and the Sappho of my own poem. Feeling persists through the fragmentariness, in both poets, in the most extraordinary way.'

Janet Paisley

Janet Paisley is a poet, writer and playwright whose poetry collections include *Alien Crop* (Chapman, 1996), and *Reading the Bones* (Canongate, 1999). She lives near Falkirk.

Don Paterson

Don Paterson's most recent collection is *The Eyes* (Faber & Faber, 1999).

Walter Perrie

Walter Perrie was born in 1949 and lives in Dunning, Strathearn. His collections of poems include *From Milady's Wood* (Scottish Cultural Press, 1997) and a recently completed collection entitled *The Light in Strathearn*.

'I like to fancy Ronsard may have passed through Dunning on his way to and from the Royal Court at Perth. When Madeleine of France married James V, Ronsard was attached to the Court for three years and returned to Scotland again later in the service of the duc d'Orleans. Mary Stuart seems to have been patroness of his first *Oeuvres Completes* in 1560 and wrote to him from her English captivity.'

Tom Pow

Tom Pow lives in Dumfries, where he teaches English. His most recent collection is *Red Letter Day* (Bloodaxe, 1996). With Hugh Bryden he runs Cacafuego Press which specialises in works marrying word and image; their first publication was *Landscapes* (1999).

Richard Price

Richard Price was born in Renfrewshire in 1966. His most recent collection is *Perfume and Petrol Fumes* (Diehard, 1999); he is a co-editor of *Southfields* magazine.

'The Gallant Weaver' is a favourite for obvious personal reasons – the song is based in the weaving county of Renfrewshire where I grew up – but also because there is something heroic and joyful about the female singer's persistence – despite the risk to her dowry or 'tocher' and to a settled future. The weavers in the broad valleys round rivers such as the Cart had a reputation for dangerous independent thinking.'

Alan Riach

Alan Riach is Associate Professor of English at the University of Waikato, New Zealand. He is the editor of Hugh MacDiarmid's *Collected Works* and author of two critical books on MacDiarmid. His poetry is collected in *This Folding Map* (Auckland University Press, 1990), *An Open Return* (Untold Books, 1991) and *First and Last Songs* (Chapman, 1995).

'I once mentioned MacDiarmid's allusion to the Eas-Coul-aulin to Norman MacCaig. "Don't trust him," MacCaig said. "He'd never been there!" Maybe not, but when my wife and I went out on the boat from Kylesku to see the Falls, Willie Watson told us the legend MacDiarmid refers to. "Oh aye, it's true. That's the place. That's the place, right enough."

Robin Robertson

Robin Robertson's most recent collection is *A Painted Field*, (Picador, 1997).

Ian Stephen

Ian Stephen was born in 1955, and has lived for many years in Stornoway, Isle of Lewis. His poetry and prose were featured in the first pocketbook, *Green Waters*. Norman Malcolm Macdonald was born in 1927 and raised in Tong (Isle of Lewis), where he now lives. He has published novels, plays and poetry.

Gael Turnbull

Gael Turnbull was born in Edinburgh in 1923, where he now lives after spending much of his life in England, the United States and Canada. His most recent book is *For Whose Delight* (Mariscat, 1995).

'I first knew this poem from *Seventeen Poems for Sixpence* (1943) and certain phrases became part of the permanent anthology I carry about in my head.'

Christopher Whyte

Christopher Whyte began learning Gaelic at the age of 20 and published his first poems in the language 15 years later in 1987. His first collection, *Uirsgeul/Myth*, was published by Gairm in 1991. He has also published three novels in English. His poem is translated into English by Gavin Bowd, who lectures in the Department of French Literature at the University of St Andrews.

'Gil de Biedma's combination of raunchiness with understatement recalls W. H. Auden, whom he so much admired. There is no querulousness in his work, no sense of complaint or being a victim, none of the existential 'lostness' which has so often troubled me.'

Index of Authors

Acknowledgements

Thanks are due to the following copyright holders for permission to reproduce the poems in this collection. While every effort has been made to trace and credit copyright holders, the Publishers will be glad to rectify any oversights in any future editions.

MARION ANGUS: 'The Faithful Heart', from *Selected Poems*, (© Serif Books, 1950); JOHN BERRYMAN: 'Dream Song', from *The Dream Songs* (© Faber & Faber, 1990); NINA CASSIAN: 'Temptation', from *Call Yourself Alive?*, (© Forest Books, 1988); MENG CHIAO: 'Impromptu', from *Poems of the Late T'ang*, translated by A. C. Graham (© Penguin Classics, 1965) © A. C. Graham, 1965, reproduced by permission of Penguin Books; KATE CLANCHY: 'Heliograph', from *Samarkand*, (© Macmillan, 1999); PADRAIC COLUM: 'She Moved Through The Fair', from *The Poet's Circuits*, (© Oxford University Press, 1960); HART CRANE: 'The Harbor Dawn', from *Hart Crane: The Complete Poems*, edited by Marc Simon. (© Liveright Publishing Corporation, New York, 1933, 1958, 1966. © Marc Simon, 1986. Used by permission of Liveright Publishing Corporation); ROBERT CREELEY: 'The Immoral Proposition' and 'Love Comes Quietly', from *Poems 1950-1965*, (© Marion Boyars, 1966); G. F. DUTTON: 'Violets', first published in *Camp One*. ALLISON FUNK: 'The Deer', first published in *Shenandoah*; ROBERT GARIOCH: 'Ghaisties', from *Complete Poetical Works*, (© Canongate Books, 1983); JAIME GIL DE BIEDMA: 'Vals del Aniversario', from *Las persona del verbo*, (© Editorial Seix Barral, Barcelona, 1992); JOHN GLENDAY: 'The Leaving', from *Undark*, (© Peterloo Poets, 1995); GEORGE CAMPBELL HAY: 'Briodal Mathar', from *Four Points of a Saltire*, first published Gordon Wright Reprographica, 1970, courtesy of the W. L. Lorimer Trust 1999/2000; George Campbell Hay's *Collected Poems*, Polygon, 1999; TED HUGHES: 'Bridestones, West Yorkshire', from *The Remains of Elmet*, (© Faber & Faber, 1979); BRIAN JOHNSTONE: 'Pomegranate', from *Pomegranate* by Jean Johnstone; NORMAN MACCAIG: 'No Choice', 'True

Ways Of Knowing', 'Poem For A Goodbye' from *Collected Poems*, (©
Chatto & Windus/Random House, 1985); EWAN MACCOLL: 'Joy of
Living' is included on the CD *Black and White* (Cooking Vinyl CD 038);
HUGH MACDIARMID: 'Of My First Love', from *The Complete Poems of
Hugh MacDiarmid Vol. II* (© Carcanet Press Ltd., 1985) and *Selected Poems
of Hugh MacDiarmid* (© New Directions Publishing Corp.); NORMAN
MALCOLM MACDONALD: 'Mor', from *Fad*, (© Buidhean Foillseachaidh
nan Eilean); ANTONIO MACHADO: 'Los Ojos' from *Poesias Completas*
(Espasa Calpe 1980), reproduced courtesy of D. José Rollán Riesco
representative of the heirs of the author; JAMES MCGONIGAL: 'Eye of
the Beholder', first published in *New Writing Scotland 9*, (Association for
Scottish Literary Studies, 1991); SORLEY MACLEAN: 'Poems To Eimhir'
(IV), translated by Iain Crichton Smith, first published in *Poems To
Eimhir*, (Northern House, 1971), reproduced courtesy of the estates of
Sorley Maclean and Iain Crichton Smith; PABLO NERUDA: Sonnet XLVI,
from *Cien Sonetos de Amor*, translated by John Manson, first published in
The Scotsman, 18/9/93; 'Your Breast Is Enough', from *Twenty Love Poems
and a Song of Despair*, (© Jonathan Cape/Random House, 1975); DON
PATERSON: 'The Eyes', from *The Eyes*, (© Faber & Faber, 1999);
DOMHNALL RUADH: 'An Eala Bhan/The Fair Swan' from *Domhnall
Ruadh Choruna* (© Comann Eachoriadh-uibhist a Tuath Tigh
Chearsabhagh). IAIN CRICHTON SMITH: 'The World's a Minefield'
from *Love Poems and Elegies*, (© Victor Gollancz, 1972); *Collected Poems*,
(© Carcanet Press, 1992) 'Tha Thu Aigeann M' Inntinn' (Scottish
International, no.4, 1968); WILLIAM SOUTAR: 'The Tryst', from *The
Poems of William Soutar*, (Scottish Academic Press, 1988) © by permission
The Trustees of the National library of Scotland; WILLIAM CARLOS
WILLIAMS: 'Address', from *Collected Poems Vol. II* (© Carcanet Press,
1988) and *Collected Poems 1939-1962 Vol. II* (© 1955 William Carlos
Williams; © New Directions Publishing Corp.).

pocketbooks

Summer 1998

01   GREEN WATERS
      An anthology of boats and voyages, edited by Alec Finlay;
      featuring poetry, prose and visual art by Ian Stephen,
      Ian Hamilton Finlay, Graham Rich.
      ISBN 0 9527669 2 2; paperback, 96pp, colour illustrations, reprinting.

Spring 2000

02   ATOMS OF DELIGHT
      An anthology of Scottish haiku and short poems, edited with an
      Introduction by Alec Finlay, and a Foreword by Kenneth White.
      ISBN 0 7486 6275 8; paperback, 208pp, £7.99.

03   LOVE FOR LOVE
      An anthology of love poems, edited by John Burnside and
      Alec Finlay, with an Introduction by John Burnside.
      ISBN 0 7486 6276 6; paperback, 200pp, £7.99.

04   WITHOUT DAY
      An anthology of proposals for a new Scottish Parliament, edited
      by Alec Finlay, with an introduction by David Hopkins. *Without
      Day* includes an Aeolus CD by William Furlong.
      ISBN 0 7486 6277 4; paperback with CD, 184pp, £7.99 (including VAT).

Autumn 2000

05   WISH I WAS HERE
        A multicultural, multilingual poetry anthology, edited by
        Kevin MacNeil and Alec Finlay, with an Aeolus CD.

06   WILD LIFE
        Hamish Fulton, walking artist, works made in the Cairngorms.
        Wild Life includes an Aeolus CD.

07   A DAY BOOK
        David Shrigley

Available through all good bookshops.

Book trade orders to:
Scottish Book Source, 137 Dundee Street, Edinburgh EH11 1BG.

Copies are also available from:
Morning Star Publications, Canongate Venture (5), New Street,
Edinburgh EH8 8BH.

Website: www.pbks.co.uk